UPLAND SALADO ICONOGRAPHY
AND RELIGIOUS CHANGE

UPLAND SALADO ICONOGRAPHY
AND RELIGIOUS CHANGE

Charmion R. McKusick

Arizona Archaeological Society

April 2017

The Arizona Archaeologist

April 2017   Number 41

The cover drawing shows a Tonto Polychrome jar found in the Globe-Miami area, and currently on display in the Bullion Plaza Museum, Miami, Arizona. The designs depict a horn worm on the shoulder and body of the jar, and a Hawk Moth just below the lip, at the upper-left. This worm is the prototype for Southwestern horned serpents with forward-curving horns. See the section titled "Feathered and/or Horned Serpents" for more information. Drawing by Charmion R. McKusick. Overall cover design by Jim Carlson.

This volume edited by Alan Ferg. Peer review by Peter J. Pilles, Jr., Forest Archaeologist, Coconino National Forest

Bill Burkett, *Arizona Archaeologist* Series Editor

ISBN 978-0-939071-76-0

Published by the Arizona Archaeological Society, Inc.
P.O. Box 9665
Phoenix, AZ 85068-9665

www.AzArchSoc.org

Members of the Arizona Archaeological Society, at the time of publication, have the option of receiving a free hardcopy. Members can also download PDF versions, and, when available, Kindle ebook versions of the *Arizona Archaeologist* from the Member-Only page of the Society's website.

Abstract

The Upland Salado of the Globe-Miami area in central Arizona are considered members of the Casas Grandes Trade Network, in contrast to the Tonto Basin Salado who were members of the Hohokam Trade Network. A Kayenta immigrant population is documented at Besh-Ba-Gowah. Iconography is followed from the Old World, through the Early Postclassic International Symbol Set and Mimbres figurative pottery design, to A.D. 1440s Salado ceramic symbolism. Mesoamerican god cults, and the psychoactive medicinals associated with them, are discussed in relationship to religious change and the local termination of the Salado phenomenon.

Keywords: Salado, iconography, Southwestern Indian religion, psychoactive substances, migration.

Table of Contents

List of Figures

List of Tables

Acknowledgements

This book began in 1949, at the University of Arizona, when Frances Gillmor, my essay instructor, introduced me to the beauties of the Nahuatl language and the codices which illustrated its complexities. The process continued in the fall of 1950, when I began courses in Southwest Indian art and religion, and primitive art and religion, taught by Clara Lee Tanner, who eventually became my Honors Professor. In 1951 I married Robert McKusick who had grown up next door to Besh-Ba-Gowah. Irene Vickrey and her husband, and Ernst Antev and Deric O'Bryan of the Gila Pueblo archaeological group were all dear McKusick family friends. When Robert brought me home to meet the family, the first activity on his list was to climb through the fence to the overgrown excavation, and lead me on Irene Vickrey's tour, with word-for-word lecture. Another Besh-Ba-Gowah neighbor, the late John Woody, regaled me with the same word-for-word account, adding a few additional essential bits of information.

March 2011 at the home of Señora Conchita Mancinas in Barranca del Cobre, Chihuahua, Mexico. Sra. Mancinas, a Tarahumara *curandera,* is at center-left, diagnosing Robert McKusick at center-right. Sra. Mancinas made critical contributions to my understanding of traditional uses of psychoactive substances. Robert, who passed away on June 20, 2016, was always a supportive driving force in all my Salado researches.

As the years went by, Jon Nathan Young excavated the Hagen Site and I led the excavation of the south end of Gila Pueblo. By 1997, Jon and I realized we were getting older, and prepared *The Gila Pueblo Salado* to document the sites before we, like Vickrey, died unexpectedly. We were not completely happy with the interpretations we were able to suggest. The facts were correct, but they did not always seem coherent.

After 20 more years of study, the situation is becoming clearer, mostly as a result of the efforts of a lot of helpful people. First, it has been invaluable to have feedback from my husband Robert, and my daughter Kathleen Condit, both of whom participated in the 1971-1973 excavation of Gila Pueblo. Although Harold Sterling Gladwin had long since retired to California, he provided invaluable advice during the 1970s excavation of Gila Pueblo by telephone. He assured me that the horrific slaughter we were uncovering was representative of his findings in the remainder of the pueblo. The staff of the Arizona State Museum was particularly helpful: Alan Ferg provided me with copies of Vickrey's extensive notes and photographs, and has procured many publications for me; Mike Jacobs provided scans of artifacts from which I was able to prepare illustrations; and Barnet Pavao-Zuckerman provided copies of osteological reconstruction tables. Edward R. Colyott, Sr., retired Tonto National Monument ranger, assisted with the Paleo-Indian Period, and Vorsila L. Bohrer with the Archaic Period. My grandson, Thierry Condit, has found numerous sources online, and has remedied many computer problems. Amadeo Rea and Philip Smith assisted with the view to the south. Richard Fisher and Sra. Conchita Mancinas assisted with Mexican perspectives. Philip DeMario has loaned and given me a mountain of books on shamanism, iconography, and psychoactive plants, as well as serving as an agent for the anonymous donation of local heirloom artifacts.

Finally, I thank William H. Doelle for reading the original version of the manuscript. It was at his urging that Alan Ferg got it out of mothballs. Many thanks go, too, to Alan for his work editing the manuscript and to Peter Pilles for his review.

This compilation of data could not have been completed without the generous assistance of the persons mentioned, and no doubt many others who I have forgotten in the 68 years since it began. I thank all of them. Any errors are, of course, mine alone. My ethnobiological and shamanistic view of Southwest archaeology is admittedly peculiar, but I hope it may stir a latent thought in some reader which will take us a little farther down the road.

In Memory of Irene Vickrey,
who took such wonderful notes
and had the foresight
to measure the human long bones *in situ*.

The breath and life force depart from the deceased, leaving only the skeleton.
(simplified from Gonzales 2012: 205)

About the Author

Charmion McKusick grew up in Waukegan, Illinois, sailing on Lake Michigan. Her ambition was to study physical anthropology, which brought her to the University of Arizona in Tucson in September of 1949.

During a summer at Point of Pines Field School in 1952, she found bird and animal bones far more interesting than human bones. Her training in bird bones came while serving as a laboratory assistant to Dr. Lyndon Lane Hargrave. Charmion's tenure at the Southwest Archeological Center included training in mammal bone identification under Thomas W. Mathews. She has identified faunal specimens from the greater Southwest and Mexico, and has special interests in Indian Domestic Turkey breeds, Mexican macaws, birds of sacrifice, iconography, and the Upland Salado people.

Charmion is also the author of "Evidences of Hereditary High Status at Gila Pueblo" (1992), in *Proceedings of the Second Salado Conference, Globe, AZ 1992,* an occasional paper of the Phoenix Chapter of the Arizona Archaeological Society; *The Gila Pueblo Salado (1997),* an Arizona Archaeological Society publication co-authored with Jon Young; *Southwest Birds of Sacrifice, Arizona Archaeologist No. 31* (2001); and "Upland Salado Resource Use" in the festschrift *Explorations in Ethnobiology: The Legacy of Amadeo Rea,* edited by Marsha Quinlan and Dana Lepofsky from the Society of Ethnobiology, University of North Texas, Denton (2013).

Introduction

Red ochre, the earliest icon considered, was used by the Neanderthals, *Homo sapiens neanderthalenis*, 42,000 years ago (Marshack n.d.). Marshack provides evidence that many icons still in use were first brought to Eurasia by modern man, *Homo sapiens sapiens*, as much as 50,000 years ago in some areas. Presumably they were carried to the New World by the Pre-Paleo-Indians and Paleo-Indians, and persisted in use among female midwives and male hunting shamans through the late Archaic.

McGuire (2011: 23-49) summarizes the introduction into the Mexican Northwest/North American Southwest of cosmologies, rituals, and symbols accompanying the introduction of farming and the Uto-Aztecan language. To this assemblage I would add the introduction of the Small Indian Domestic Turkey phenotype (McKusick 1986; McKusick 2001: 43-49). Boone and Smith (2003: 186-193) identify an Early Postclassic International Symbol Set as an indicator of a Quetzalcoatl Cult dating from the tenth to the thirteenth centuries, a time period which encompasses the production of Mimbres Classic Black-on-white (Mimbres B/w), Mimbres Polychrome, and the earliest Salado polychrome (Roosevelt Red Ware) pottery types. This iconography persisted in southeastern Arizona and southwestern New Mexico, resulting in a greater resemblance of the art of this region to the earlier Maya art, than to the later Aztec art.

Crown (1994) explores design elements depicted on Salado polychrome pottery and concludes that they are expressions of an ideology involving an Archaic Period "flower world" concept, and also elements of local manifestations of later, farming-period Mesoamerican god cults. I considered these same god cults from an ethno-ornithological perspective, and arrived at a similar conclusion (McKusick 2001).

This consideration of iconography includes elements found in Crown's examination of Salado in general, but concentrates on Upland Salado as separate from the Tonto Basin Salado. Crary, Germick, and Golio (1994), present an excellent summary of the development of local sites of all sizes. The history of the excavation of the pueblos is detailed by Hohmann (1990). The 1930s and 1980s excavations of Besh-Ba-Gowah are summarized in Vickrey (1939), Hohmann (1992b), Hohmann and Adams (1992), and Hohmann, Germick, and Adams (1992). The Pinal Site, an outlier of Besh-Ba-Gowah which was destroyed by power line construction and pothunting, is reported in Boggess, Ajeman, Gilman, and Bozarth (1992). A brief paragraph on Gladwin's 1930s excavation of Gila Pueblo mentioning a kiva with a bench, and similarities to Point of Pines, is found in McGregor (1965: 423). The report on Shiner's National Park Service excavation of one room at Gila Pueblo was published in 1961. Young's 1968 salvage excavation of the Hagen Site and my 1971-1973 Eastern Arizona College excavation of a ceremonial/redistribution complex at Gila Pueblo are reported in McKusick and Young (1997). Information from Ferg's completion of one room of this excavation is included herein. The Gila Pueblo excavation provided information on Mesoamerican God Cults, which is covered in McKusick 2001. Upland Salado ethnobiology and resource usage may be found in McKusick 2013.

This examination of icons focuses on those which would have been understood and used by the prehistoric inhabitants of the Globe-Miami Highlands of eastern Arizona at all time periods. These include the Paleo-Indian campsite underlying Gila Pueblo, the late Archaic Period hunter-gatherers, the Hohokam pit house villages, and the Upland Salado Pueblos. This is also an attempt to understand the world view and changing religious practices of the inhabitants of Besh-Ba-Gowah, Gila Pueblo, and their outliers, as they evolved from the construction of the pueblos, ca. A.D. 1225, to their destruction in the 1440s. Site closing activities, which were not understood fully enough to report in McKusick and Young (1997), are detailed. In addition, possible models for the circumstances surrounding the destruction of the pueblos, and the fate of their populations are considered.

1—Icons Brought By the Paleo-Indians

In September of 1949, when I arrived at the University of Arizona, the view of early man in North America was just that, "Early Man." Humans were presented as having walked here across Beringia, a vast, 1000-mile-wide expanse of land which joined Asia and Alaska, 25,000 to 40,000 years ago, perhaps even 100,000 years ago. Leaving that Anthropology 101 lecture I had a vivid picture in my mind of proto-humans scampering empty-headed and empty-handed, naked and barefoot, through the snow, heading as fast as possible for warmer climes. There was no description offered of their way of life, only unending arguments between the "Diffusionists" and the "Independent Inventionists" about how these innocents abroad in the New World came by various stone tool types. This went on for years, with no consideration of what people were doing to make a living between the time they arrived and the time their descendants turned up in the Southwest Culture Area as the Basketmakers and the Ancestral Pueblo Peoples.

Looking back on this situation from a perspective of over 60 years in archaeology, I realize that this version of Anthropology 101, and the archaeology and anthropology courses which followed it, were products of a period of reorganization of the whole field of archaeology, which had undergone a hiatus during World War II. There was an attempt to instill in the student some semblance of logic and scientific method, and "theories" were to be formulated and "proved" or "disproved." In today's archaeology, new questions can be asked, some of which can be answered by excavation, by re-examination of excavation reports from many years ago, or by reading published compilations of symposium papers by current authorities in various interpretive fields such as ethnobotany, ethnozoology, and linguistics. Now, models can be formulated which can be put forth for consideration by others, holes poked in them, pieces added to them, and major renovations undertaken. As long as someone is working feverishly to salvage a site which is about to be destroyed, as long as someone is drudging through file cards which were written before they were born, as long as someone is pulling macaw bones out of bags in which they have remained untouched since their grandparents were small children, we will have more and more pieces of the puzzle. The picture gets better, and brighter, and much more fun.

Old World Beginnings

My approach to archaeology is as an ethnobiologist. I am not comfortable formulating models which do not involve being able to hold actual bones of biological organisms in my hands, including human bones. In spite of the visions of pre-Modern Humans in North America some held in years past, absolutely no bones of "Early Man" as a biological organism have been discovered in the New World. All ancient bones, including persons of Pre-Paleo-Indian and Paleo-Indian Cultures, are those of fully modern *Homo sapiens sapiens*. This fact leads me to wonder, as did the "Diffusionists" and "Independent Inventionists," what elements of culture were available in the Old World for migrants to select from, to make up the tool kit they brought to the New World?

Following the 1972 publication of *The Roots of Civilization,* Alexander Marshack prepared a catalogue called *Ice Age Art* (n.d.), for an exhibition of photographs and artifacts at The Academy of Natural Sciences of Philadelphia. The exhibit encompassed five Old World areas, each quite different from the others in environmental resources:

Franco-Cantabrian, West European, ca. 37,000 -12,000 years ago
This culture flourished in the protected valleys of rivers flowing from the mountains of southern France and Northern Spain to the Atlantic Ocean. Cliffs of limestone provided rock shelters where hunters lived, and caves where they made paintings, engravings, and carvings. This was a colder area with herds of reindeer and wooly mammoth.

Mediterranean, Italian, East Spanish, ca. 24,000 -10,500 years ago
The river valleys draining to, and fronting on, the Mediterranean Sea had fewer cold weather herd animals. Animal art is not as rich. Small stones bearing painted and engraved serpentine or geometric designs predominate, but early "Venus" figures are reminiscent of those found in the remainder of Europe.

Czechoslovakian/Moravian, Central European, ca. 30,000-12,000 years ago
Large herds of reindeer, mammoth, horse, and bison inhabited the rolling permafrost hills and plains. The hunters lived in mammoth bone huts. Female and animal images included the same subject matter as Western Europe, but were rendered in a different style, one that spread eastward, toward Russia.

Upper Ukrainian, East European, ca. 30,000-12,000 years ago
The Upper Dnieper River system flowed through permafrost steppe. Mammoth bones provided material for huts, and were burned for warmth. Female images similar to those of France, Austria, and Czechoslovakia were carved from mammoth ivory. The eastern Asiatic style of carving and decoration continued to evolve. Although the people were reindeer and mammoth hunters, they produced little animal art.

Lake Baikal, Central Siberian, ca. 22,000-12,000 years ago
Hunters of mammoth and reindeer, classed as Mongoloid, made the same categories of artifacts, including female figurines, animal images, pendants, signs, and symbols as their contemporaries in the west without apparent European contact.

Neanderthals, *Homo sapiens neanderthalenis,* while not the earliest *Homo sapiens* in the Northern Hemisphere, flourished from Europe to China as early as 120,000 years ago. They lived in small family groups, harvesting big game with thrusting spears tipped with beautifully engineered stone points struck from a pre-form with a single blow. Their sites have not produced artifacts suitable for processing plant foods (Bosveld 2009: 49). Therefore, Bosveld's model is one in which the entire group concentrated upon hunting. Since the human digestive system is not able to process large quantities of raw meat, roasting is their most probable method of food preparation. The very small numbers of Neanderthals, over the vast period of time in which they dominated Eurasian prehistory, suggests that they were not out poking mammoths in the side with their thrusting spears, which would have led to their immediate demise, but rather were hunting young, disabled, or old animals opportunistically, or even scavenging(Adovasio, Soffer, and Page 2007:180).

Jumbled bones of a cannibalized Neanderthal family band were found at Sidrón Cave in northern Spain. There were three males, three females, and six children. Mitochondrial DNA identified the three males as related members of the same family. The women were not. This suggests a patrilocal social structure where women leave their families and join the husband's family (Patel 2011: 14). According to Marshack (n.d.), between 70,000 and 37,000 years ago Neanderthals had ritual burials, and wore pendants made of teeth and bone. Their first known use of red ochre was during the Mousterian Period, 42,000 years ago, at Tala, Hungary.

Bosveld (2009: 49) accepted that fully modern man, *Homo s. sapiens,* entered Eurasia from Africa about 50,000 years ago. Neanderthals disappeared by 30-28,000 years ago. This 20,000 year period of co-existence leaves us with many questions. One factor which has come to light is that *Homo s. sapiens* sites contain equipment for processing plant foods, such as seeds. Therefore, Bosveld's model for Cro-Magnon economy involves division of labor wherein women and children gather within walking range of the dwelling place, whereas men may range farther afield to hunt. There is no evidence that Neanderthals ever used anything but the thrusting spear, but Cro-Magnons used lighter casting spears, propelled by a spear-thrower, a device which extends the operative length of the human arm, thereby imparting great velocity to the projectile (Bosveld 2009: 49).

Papagianni and Morse (2013: 10–13, 18, 24–25, 48–49, 73–75,103–104, 132–135, 169, 174) present a more expansive model. Briefly, they propose a human, probably *Homo heidelbergensis,* in Africa and Europe 600,000 YA (years ago). DNA indicates that Modern Humans and Neanderthals shared a common ancestor 500,000 YA. From *H. heidelbergensis,* Neanderthals evolved in Europe, early *H. sapiens* evolved in Africa, and Denisovans may have evolved in Siberia. By 250,000 YA, Neanderthals were in Africa, Europe, and Asia. About 130,000 YA, early *H. sapiens* moved north out of Africa. Around 100,000 YA, both Neanderthals and early *H, sapiens* began to bury their dead in caves and rock shelters, both had language, and both were ambush hunters in a wooded landscape. Neanderthals produced the Levalloisian tool complex, and early *H. sapiens* produced the Aurignacian tool complex. At 45,000 YA, modern humans, *H. s. sapiens,* who were pursuit hunters, developed in East Africa and began to spread. By 33,000 YA, these Gravettian tool complex producers took advantage of climate change to occupy the expanding steppes where they fished the rivers and hunted migratory herd animals. By 22,000 YA, the Gravettian Culture, with its "Venus" figurines, was the only one left in Europe.

It is unlikely that anyone would question the ability of either Neanderthals or Cro-Magnons to kill deer or horse-sized prey with the equipment they had, or to slay a hibernating cave bear for that matter, but could either of them have killed an able-bodied mammoth? If a dart projected from a spear thrower hit an elephant in its thin-skinned armpit, as the foreleg stretched forward to take a step, the point and foreshaft could, and did in some cases, pass into the lung cavity where massive bleeding caused the animal's death. I doubt that this was an everyday event.

Many of the most beautiful artifacts left by the Upper Paleolithic peoples of Eurasia were made from mammoth bone and ivory, but there was no need to hunt for these raw materials. This bone and ivory was, and is still, readily available in many locations, especially frozen in the tundra, where rivers annually cut through and thaw deposits laid down thousands of years before man arrived on the scene. Deposits from the Berelekh River mammoth cemetery above the

Arctic Circle in northeastern Yakutia, contain fish scales and the remains of streambed mosses indicating that mammoths perished annually when they ventured onto thin ice, were caught in spring floods, or fell into boggy areas in search of vegetation, producing vast accumulations of bones and ivory (Stone 2001: 36-39).

It is highly unlikely that either Neanderthals or Cro-Magnons brought mammoths to the point of extinction. The end of the Pleistocene Epoch, about 11,500 years ago, was caused by a change in weather patterns over a brief period of a few decades. Huge areas of the Northern Hemisphere, which had been the cold, dry grasslands of the mammoth steppe, were suddenly subjected to summer rain and winter snow, which covered the sedges and mosses on which mammoths fed. Large mammals, which eat immense amounts of food daily, do not do well in a seasonal climate; indeed they are now found only in areas of tropical climate where a stable food supply is available year round (Stone 2001: 9).

During the 20-30,000 years of their co-existence, how did Neanderthals and Cro-Magnons get along, and did they interbreed? Considering that Cro-Magnons were at a reproductive advantage because of their improved technology and the flexibility afforded by division of labor between hunting and gathering, it is surprising that Neanderthals were not killed off, absorbed, or out-competed sooner. Neanderthal bones found at Moula-Guercy, near the Rhone River in southeastern France, have butchering marks which indicate Neanderthals were eating other Neanderthals. Injury to a rib of a Neanderthal male from Shanidar 3, a cave in the Near East, appears to have been made by a casting spear wielded by a modern human. Jawbones from a Neanderthal child and a modern human found in the cave at Les Rois in southwestern France, dating about 30,000 years ago, have stone tool marks which are the same as those left on nearby reindeer jaws when the tongues were cut out during the butchering process. Thus, we have Neanderthals eating Neanderthals, modern humans eating Neanderthals, and persons unknown eating both Neanderthals and modern humans at the same time. Whether the coexistence of these groups was cordial or not, DNA studies indicate that the Cro-Magnons out competed the Neanderthals on the one hand, and absorbed them on the other (Bosveld 2009: 48). Modern Humans and Neanderthals co-existed in the Near East for 20-30,000 years. Both groups shared descent from a common ancestor, diverged, and then experienced limited interbreeding. The result is that modern human populations outside Africa still carry an average of 2 percent of Neanderthal genes, and a little less than 2 percent of Denisovan genes (Neimark 2011: 55; National Geographic DNA studies).

More to the point than our genetic makeup is our cultural heritage. If the Neanderthals contributed the use of red ochre and burial of the dead, and early *H. sapiens,* added jewelry, the Cro-Magnons still brought a lot of other cultural items with them when they arrived in Eurasia. The complex is so widely distributed through time and space, and through such a diversity of environments ranging from the Riviera to the Siberian Tundra, that Marshack (n.d.) has come to consider a model indicating that this cultural complex was common to the Eurasian immigrants before they arrived. Stone Age Art is the most conspicuous element of this cultural tool kit. Artistic expression is largely determined by gallery space, so great murals are limited to cave walls, and where there is nothing but tundra, art is executed on small objects of ivory or bone.

Utilitarian objects included thrusting spears, and darts and harpoons launched from spear throwers. The most beautiful stone artifacts were large, finely flaked laurel-leaf-shaped projectile points. Hides were dressed with stone, bone, and ivory tools. Clothes were fashioned with bone and ivory awls and needles. The 26,000 year old Dolní Věstonice site contained an ivory loom batten as well as burned evidence of loom-woven textiles, nets, string bags, and free-standing baskets woven in eight different twining techniques (Adovasio, Soffer, and Page 2007: 181-184). Housing ranged from tents in rock shelters in Western Europe, to 22,000 year-old skin-covered huts framed with mammoth tusks and bones anchored in walls made from the stacked lower jaw bones of immature mammoths on the permafrost tundra in Siberia (Time-Life 1995: 1).

From art, and from actual molds of garments in clay, we know that Ice Age people wore clothes made from furs sewn with awls and needles, and from whip-stitched fiber cloth made by woven and non-woven methods. These include head bands, netting snoods, coiled basket hats, caps, wrist bands, bracelets, necklaces, beaded shirts, buttons, and finger rings. Recently discovered depictions show men and women wearing gowns, head bands, and caps; women with coiffures, string aprons, and tattoos; women praying; and men dancing, playing flutes, with costumes, and with beards. Carved ivory portraits of specific individuals exist. A female portrait, dated at 26,000 years ago, and that of a man, were both found at Dolní Věstonice, Czechoslovakia. That of a woman was found at Malta, Central Siberia (Marshack 1988: 478-481; Marshack n.d.: 12).

All ages and both genders took part in ceremonies. Bare footprints in ceremonial caves include men, women, and children. Whether these folk had laid aside their footgear because of the sacredness of the area, which is the case in many cultures, or had done so to save them from becoming wet in the clay, is, and may well remain, a point of conjecture. One sprayed pigment double hand print, in the cave of Gargas, registers the hand of an infant held by the wrist by the hand of an adult wearing a sleeve (Marshak n.d.:13-14).

The earliest human specialist is now thought to be the midwife. This position in society is known to exist among pre-humans even before the advent of *Homo sapiens,* because the head of the offspring of hominids must turn in a narrow, convoluted, birth canal from a side-facing to a back-facing orientation in order to pass through the pelvis (compare Adovasio, Soffer, and Page 2007: 64-71). Unassisted births are possible, but are dangerous both to the mother and to the offspring. An early acknowledgement in Old World art of the importance of the childbearing period in a woman's life is the "Venus" figure. This category of ivory and bone carvings and fired clay figurines emphasizes large hips and buttocks, huge, pendulous breasts, and a prominent abdomen. Conversely, arms are stylized, legs are tapering and may lack feet, heads are bent, and faces are undifferentiated. "Venus" figures were produced from about 32,000 to 24,000 years ago from France to the Ukraine. Coiled and twined basketry caps, hairnets, and snoods or coiffures may be depicted, as may be cords, bracelets, and tattoos, but the most important attribute is the presence of the string apron, as seen on the back view of the Venus of Lespugue (Marshack n.d.: 3-15; Schuster and Carpenter 1996: Figure 645). This curious garment, while rendered in great detail on nude female figures, is not apparent in clay impressions of clothing found in Upper Paleolithic burials. Therefore, it may have been worn on ceremonial occasions, or may be an undergarment worn by women of child-bearing age which was concealed in cold climates by their outer clothing. Pringle (2010: 33-34) documents the string skirt as an undergarment of the well-preserved mummy of the 4,000 year old "Beauty of Xiaohe" from the Tarim Basin in Northwestern China. The string skirt was also worn as an undergarment by women of child-bearing years in Europe, not only throughout the Bronze Age, but in some areas, such as Ireland, even into the nineteenth century. Turning to the North American Southwest, in the early ll00s, string aprons were worn by women of the Mimbres Valley, New Mexico as an undergarment, or as their only garment. At Gila Pueblo, the string apron was worn adorned with a shell bead stomacher at ca. A.D. 1440 as a ceremonial garment. Among modern Western Pueblo groups it survives as the "rain sash," woven by men for brides to wear at their wedding and at their funeral (Figure 1). It appears to have served as an icon for the gushing flow of amniotic fluid which precedes birth.

Two fragmentary flutes made from swan wing bones were recovered from Geiβenklöstlere, in southern Germany. At nearby Höhle Fels, a flute carved from mammoth ivory, dating between 37,000 and 30,000 years old, is at present the oldest known musical instrument (Curry 2007: 30-31). Two intact flutes, with four holes above and six below have been found, one in France and one in the Ukraine. A Ukrainian mammoth bone hut also yielded a six-instrument percussion ensemble. They are made of mammoth bone, each with a different tone. Bull roarers made of bone or ivory are recovered, but I have not found records of surviving drums, rattles, or musical rasps.

Anthropologists tend to divide time into three linear categories. The first is the Mythical, the Dawn Time of Primal-Flux, of formlessness and void, when animals could talk, when forms could change, ebb and flow, and take on each other's attributes, a time when things were not as they are now. After Creation, which, in the anthropologists' minds at least, solidified this reality, comes the second period, the Legendary. This period has some basis in fact. An example is the vast body of Hopi Migration Stories, which contain both actual places, and semi-supernatural culture heroes and events. Third is the Visible World of time and place in which the anthropologists live today. These concepts of a present time and a present place are essential to getting on the commuter train on schedule, but are not particularly useful to a shaman.

The term "shaman" represents, in the most literal sense, a Siberian male or female practitioner whose function is to preserve the balance between the Visible World and the much larger, more inclusive, and more enduring, Unseen Universe. In the Paleolithic Period this could be manifested in physical or emotional healing, in increasing fertility of man or of prey animals, or in success in hunting. Anthropologists tend to differentiate between the shaman and the priest, defining the shaman as one who works independently for the benefit of individuals, and the priest as one who belongs to a religious organization, and works in concert with others of that organization for the community as a whole. The anthropologists tend to regard the role of the priest as "safe," because failure to perform successfully can be blamed on the "bad thoughts" of someone in the community, rather than upon the efforts of the priest. Priesthoods are generally associated with a farming state of cultural development, but shamans may function at any level of cultural development. The priest is constrained by the limitations of traditional practice, and works within a structure. He attends to the needs of the community by leading corporate prayer for rain and fertility, and serves the needs of the individual by conducting ceremonies marking the various stages of life from birth to death. The shaman, on the other hand, is equally

Figure 1. String Apron/Amniotic Fluid Icon. <u>Top-left</u>: string back apron worn by the Venus of Lespugue, mammoth ivory, ca. 25,000 B.C., after Schuster and Carpenter 1996: 272, Figure 645 and Prideaux 1973: 98-99. <u>Top-center</u>: a woman has laid aside her belt and apron while giving birth, Mimbres Classic B/w, after Cosgrove and Cosgrove 1932: Plate 225. <u>Top-right</u>: string apron worn as an undergarment, Mimbres Classic B/w, after Brody 1977: 161, Figure 101. <u>Bottom-left</u>: string apron worn with shell bead stomacher, Mimbres Classic B/w, after Bradfield 1931: Plate 79, No. 364. <u>Bottom-middle</u>: Chalchihuitlicue seated on birthing stool with two infants carried on a stream of amniotic fluid, Codex Borbonicus, 16th century Aztec, after Miller and Taube, 1993: 61. <u>Bottom-right</u>: Snow Maiden katsina wearing rain sash, woodcarving by Stetson Lomayestewa, after Schaafsma 1994 and 2000: cover.

comfortable in the Visible World and in the Unseen Universe, and is attached to neither. She or he works beyond limitation, where the Primal Flux still exists, where animals still talk, and where shapes still change.

The shaman depicted in Ice Age art is always male, is generally costumed in animal skins, and is often dancing and playing a flute made from the wing bone of a large bird like a swan, or a crane (Figure 2). Along with the shaman we have the reality that midwives have been around much longer than modern mankind, and we have the "Venus" figures. Both male and female functionaries were apparently considered essential to survival. This leads us to the most important concept of all, Complementary Duality. There is no place for competition in this type of a society; everyone is important; everyone must do their part, or nobody will survive.

Marschack (n.d.) found that infrared photography and ultraviolet florescence brought out details of incised and carved objects which indicated ceremonial observance of the four seasons, implying understanding of the solar year. Observation of the path of the sun inescapably leads to consciousness of the seven sacred directions, North, South, East, West, Zenith (up), Nadir (down), and Center. Plaques marked with the phases of the moon, demonstrate consciousness of the lunar month. The 29.5 day lunar month is particularly interesting, as it roughly coincides with the human menstrual cycle and with the gestation period of hares and rabbits. The concept of the "Rabbit in the Moon" is found all the way around the Arctic Circle.

Another Holarctic lunar idiom is the depiction of the Maiden, the Matron, and the Crone, which mark the three phases of the visible moon. The fourth week, the dark of the moon, is a retrograde time of transition and unmaking. Venus, as the Morning Star, and as the Evening Star, was probably classed with the sun and the moon, since all three bodies are capable of casting a shadow. Still another important Holarctic cosmological unit is the group of stars which rotates around Polaris, the North Star, and never sinks beneath the horizon. Polaris, around which everything revolves, is associated with a creator concept. The constellation we call the Big Dipper is generally considered a masculine icon; and Cassiopia, opposite, is generally considered a feminine icon, like a mother and father facing each other across a hearth signified by Polaris. The identities assigned to each of these icons vary through time, place, and culture period, but the genders remain the same (Williams, Blackhorse, Stein, and Friedman 2006: 103-113).

The Settlement of the New World

The settlement of the New World happened by fits and starts. The Pre-Paleo-Indians may have arrived on both the east and west coasts of North America as beachcombers, fishermen, and hunters of maritime mammals. Some of the early folk on the west coast may have traits in common with the Ainu of the northern islands of Japan. The early laurel leaf projectile points made in North America resemble the Solutrean stonework of France in shape and technique of manufacture, and the Old Cordilleran Complex, which extends down the western coastline from the Pacific Northwest to the tip of South America, also involves large, leaf-shaped blades. At this writing it appears that the technique of leaf-shaped blade manufacture was imported from the Old World, and that basal fluting developed in North America, and then spread quickly. Fluted points are far more common from the Mississippi River Drainage eastward, than they are in the West (Malakoff 2008: 28). The main problem which besets the study of this period is that sea level is about 300 feet higher today than it was when the Pre-Paleo-Indians were gathering cockles and mussels along the shore. Boats have been in use for at least 40,000 years. Researchers are considering dates for their Pre-Paleo-Indian sites which extend back to over 20,000 years ago. One thing we can be sure of is that people managed to get around a lot more, and a lot earlier, than we tend to give them credit for.

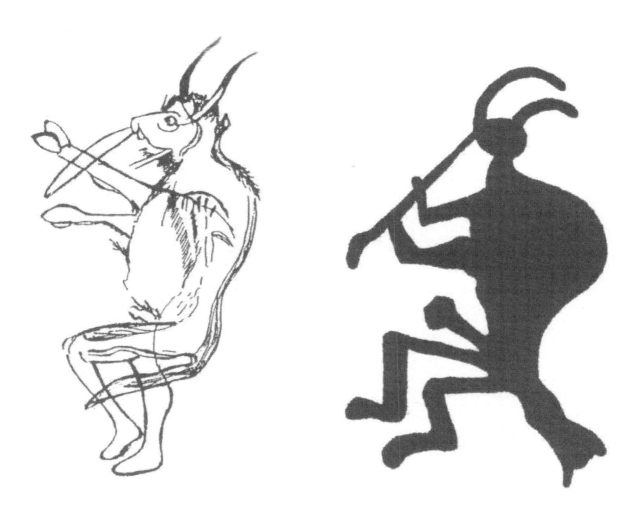

Figure 2. Phallic Musical Bison Shaman Icon. <u>Left:</u> European Bison Shaman, cave carving, dating 10,000 B.C., Dordogne, France, after van Renterghem 1995: 63, 64. <u>Right:</u> Bison Shaman/Kokopelli, petroglyph, La Cieneguilla area, after Cunkle 1993: Figure 71. Bison Shaman paraphernalia was recovered from the Jones-Miller site near Wray, Colorado, dating ca. 8,000 B.C. The Cree and Assiniboin hunted bison on foot with the aid of a pole-riding Bison Shaman in historic times (de la Haba 1976: 40-46).

The Paleo-Indians are considered to have come across Beringia from a Siberian physical stock and cultural tradition which was essentially the same on both sides of what is now the Bering Strait. They brought a knowledge of tailored skin clothing made with awls and needles; skin-covered huts; familiarity with skin-covered boats; fiber technology; the spear thrower, darts, microlith harpoons, and other hunting and fishing tools and techniques; jewelry; gambling games; and medium-sized dogs with upright ears which are descended from eastern Asiatic wolves domesticated about 16,300 years ago (Lobell and Powell 2010: 26). As modern men, who utilized plant foods, as well as hunted foods, it should not be surprising that they also brought Asiatic bottle gourds. Bottle gourds, *Lagenaria siceraria,* although not food plants, are important because they can be used for lightweight, durable, water bottles, containers, scoops, fishing floats, and musical instruments. Bottle gourds were cultivated in Peru, Florida, and Mexico between 6,000 and 8,000 B.C. (Roney and Hard 2009: 5).

They also brought midwifery and shamanism; Sun, Moon and Venus cosmology; a recognition of the stars which rotate around Polaris and are always visible; and the concept of complementary dualism. Luckert (1975) gives an excellent account of the Navajo Hunter Tradition, which he proposes as the most enduring expression of Paleo-Indian religion, and a useful example of complementary dualism. In this cosmology, Raven is not just a shaman, he is The Shaman, who solidified this creation when he burst forth into the Visible World with the sun he had stolen to illuminate it. Raven is a shape-changer who can take off his raven coat and enter the sweat lodge with earthly men. Raven is the patron of hunters. Raven's wife, the complementary female principal, is the patroness of game animals (Luckert 1975:135-136, 178; Feher Elston 1991:13-18; McKusick 2001: 25-35).

As of the summer of 2009, the consensus of Southwestern archaeologists was that the Clovis Phase of the Paleo-Indian Tradition in southern Arizona dated between 13,100 and 12,700 years ago (Holliday, Bever, and Metzler 2009: 2).

Evidence for a Clovis Phase occupation at Gila Pueblo consists of two chert projectile points with basal fluting recovered during the early 1970s excavation of part of the ceremonial-redistribution complex on the south end of the pueblo. They are similar to one Emil Haury (1975: v, 179-180) recovered from Ventana Cave. The first recovered was a cherished relic found in a medicine pouch worn on the right hip of a high-status young man killed on the roof of Room 102 about 1440, during the final destruction of the pueblo. In addition to the Clovis point, the pouch contained a chalcedony "desert rose," an obsidian nodule, a quartz crystal, and a copper bell. Native Americans of all periods have treasured surface finds of beautiful artifacts left by their forbearers.

The second fluted point was recovered on sterile beneath Room 101. The floor of the room was plastered over a substantial deposit of clean, soft, black, finely divided soil. Beneath this, the point rested next to a shallow hearth which had been scraped into the orange-brown pebble-filled hardpan which formed the top of the ridge upon which Gila Pueblo was later built. The hearth contained charcoal, and the area was littered with chert flakes and fragments of the durable lower leg bones of deer-sized artiodactyls. Paleontologists working in this area have uncovered bones of mammoths and llama-sized camelids. From the vantage point of the Gila

Pueblo ridge site, ancient hunters could have looked down the long slope to Pinal Creek and observed game moving up and down the watercourse, which flowed year round.

What Became of the Paleo-Indians?

The Clovis people seem to have been relatively few in number. The change in climate which ended the reign of the Pleistocene megafauna, such as mammoths, mastodons, and gomphotheres, also brought about a shift in human economy. Two sites, Blackwater Draw, on the eastern border of New Mexico, and Jake Bluff, in northwestern Oklahoma, yielded earlier Clovis tools deposited beneath later Folsom artifacts. Following the Pleistocene, the Great Plains expanded, extending from Canada to Texas, and from Missouri to California; they became the home of vast herds of large bison. The basal fluting of the Clovis point was extended to occupy most of both flat surfaces of the shorter blade of the Folsom point. The greater number of Folsom sites suggests an expanded population specializing in hunting enormous 3,000 pound bison. Some consider that dogs may have been used in hunting to stop bison so they could be speared with atlatl (spear thrower) darts.

Following the Folsom culture were Agate Basin, Dalton, Plainview, and Cody tool traditions which both succeeded and overlapped each other. During the time of Agate Basin tool manufacture, the climate warmed, the plains shrank, and with them the bison herds shrank. Human population also shrank. Bison were driven off cliffs, and into box canyons. Edward R. Colyott, Sr. points out that the herds were beginning to be managed (personal communication, November 2010).

The Bison Shaman of the Old World apparently continued to practice in the New World. 10,000 year old artifacts found at the Jones-Miller bison site near Wray, Colorado, included evidence of a pole-riding shaman equipped with a sacrificed raven, an antler flute, and a miniature stone point. Apparently he operated over several hunting seasons (de la Habra 1976: 40-46).

By the time of Cody tool manufacture, 8,500 to 8,000 B.C., the climate became cooler. The Great Plains expanded again, population increased, and hunters entered the Southwest in significant numbers. Specialized scrapers, punches, and awls indicate that resources were being utilized which had not been exploited previously. There were bison jumps, and bison traps with gates. The great period of bison hunting extended from 11,000 to 8,000 B.C., but bison hunting as a cultural focus continued until 1860-1880 (Edward R. Colyott, Sr., personal communication, November 2010; Holliday, Bever, and Meltzer 2009: 2, 3).

How Do You Cook a Bison?

Butchering a bison is a fairly standard process from Paleo-Indian times to those of the Spanish Entradas. First, several men are required to roll the dead bison from it side onto its haunches. After that, the butchering process may be carried out by one or two persons. As Pedro de Casteñeda's narrative of 1540-1542 relates, the skin of the bison was slit along the spine from the base of the skull to the base of the tail using a finger-sized flint fastened to a small stick. The hide was skinned from the carcass, and pulled down to each side forming a clean work surface.

Since bison hides are too large and too heavy to be used whole, cutting the skin the length of the spine was not a problem; it was simply the first step in making two half-skin robes. The "blanket of flesh" from the back was removed first, followed by the forequarters. Once the spine was well exposed, a long piece of sinew was stripped from each side of the spine, in continuous units from the base of the skull to the hocks of the hind legs. The ribs could then be broken loose from the spine and the internal organs cleanly extracted. Of great importance was the paunch filled with masticated grass. This was squeezed out and the resulting liquid, called "The Soul of the Grass," was drunk, providing an important source of vitamin C and other nutrients. After the sinew had been removed, the hind quarters could be butchered. The tongue, desirable camp meat, was removed by cutting along the inside of the lower jaws, and pulling it out through the throat. Neck meat, which was not so tender, came last of all (Hammond and Rey 1940: 26; Wheat 1967: 52; Theodore Frisbie, personal communication, 1968).

Since human digestion is not equipped to process large quantities of raw meat, it is probable that some meat was roasted over fires or cooked pit barbeque style with heated rocks. Boiling in bags with heated rocks is possible, but inefficient. Undoubtedly, the vast majority of bison meat, at all time periods, was sun dried. The point of cooking meat is to precipitate the protein so that it may be digested more easily. Drying meat also precipitates the protein. Modern humans do a lot of gathering as they go along; various herbs could be used to keep flies off the drying meat, to help preserve it, and to add flavor. Once the meat has been dried, it is much reduced in weight and bulk, and can be pounded up and stored in bags for easy transport. In 1599, Don Juan de Oñate described bands of Plains Indians traveling with harnessed, shaggy, medium-sized dogs dragging travois loaded with hundred-pound packs of dried meat and ground corn (Bolton 1916: 227).

Summary of North American Paleo-Indian Icons

The most demonstrable icons of the Paleo-Indian Period occur in pairs. The earliest are the string skirt/amniotic fluid/midwife icon and the phallic, musical Buffalo Shaman icon. More recent are raven-and-wife as patrons of the hunter and of game animals, respectively. Both sets of icons demonstrate complementary duality.

2—Icons of the Upland Archaic

The environmental abundance of upland East Central Arizona was such that the Archaic Cultural Period lasted much longer here than it did in less fortunate locations, extending until about A.D. 600. The period is characterized in the archaeological record by abundant fiber artifacts found in dry rock shelters. These include cordage and knots of many types, twined bags, rabbit-skin cord robes, baskets, sandals constructed by various techniques, and long rabbit nets. Fiber artifacts also include agave quids. These are masticated wads of agave fiber spat out after the sweet, nutritious portion of the roasted agave heart has been extracted and swallowed. As garbage, they are public domain. DNA studies of prehistoric population can be performed using agave quids from dry rock shelters without offending the sensibilities of Native American tribes (Le Blanc 2007). Stone artifacts include atlatl weights, medium to large dart points, mortars for crushing resilient foods like acorns, and flat milling stones useful for rotary grinding of small seeds with a one-handed mano.

Studies of faunal remains from Archaic sites indicate a pattern of seasonal movement to take advantage of recurring low-labor, high-calorie opportunities such as gathering fat marsh bird nestlings fallen from rookery nests, seasonal wildfowl migrations, fish spawning runs, or piñon nut harvests. From my faunal-remains viewpoint, I characterize this as Central Based Wandering. To me, this means that an Archaic Period band returned to its territory on a seasonal basis with sufficient predictability, regularity, and sense of territoriality to make it practical to leave food processing equipment near the hunting or gathering site for annual use. It also means to me that site use was sufficient to generate garbage dumps and burials.

Social anthropologists tend to view the archaic band as being made up of a dominant male, his brothers, or other close male relatives, wives born in neighboring bands, and their children. This has obvious survival value. Intensive foraging makes use of more territory than any other life style, but not every resource is available everywhere every year. The Archaic lifestyle is extremely variable. If one band suffered dearth during a given harvest, they could appeal to the neighboring band of one of the wives for permission to gather overabundant resources in their territory.

The Globe-Miami Highlands lack dry rock shelters. As a result, the only Archaic Period artifacts recovered are occasional surface finds of dart points. My students have viewed, but not touched, well preserved rabbit nets stored in rock shelters in the Cherry Creek area while deer hunting. I have also seen two atlatl weights from this area. One was a black ground steatite raven; the other was a flaked white chert cruciform (Figure 3). The use of a raven as an atlatl weight suggests a continuation of Old World and Paleo-Indian hunter tradition, which includes Raven as the patron of hunters (Luckert 1975: 135, 178; Feher-Elston 1991:13-28), and Raven's wife as the patron of game animals (Luckert 1976:136). The white cruciform is an icon of Venus as the Morning Star Warrior who drives the stars from the sky so the sun can rise (Thompson 2006: 172-173).

Figure 3. Venus as Morning Star Warrior Icon and Raven Icons. <u>Top-left:</u> Venus as Morning Star Warrior who chases the stars from the sky so the sun can come up, with Elder Brother face paint. Stars are shown around the margin of the bowl (Thompson 2006:172-173). Mimbres Polychrome, after Brody 1977: Plate 14, 71. <u>Top-right:</u> flaked white cruciform atlatl weight, Cherry Creek, Gila County, Arizona; Arizona State Museum catalog # 2002-291-1. <u>Middle-right:</u> ground black steatite raven atlatl weight, also Cherry Creek, private collection. <u>Bottom-left:</u> pictograph of an entranced shaman with bird mask and bird staff from the bottom of a 23 foot shaft at Lascaux, France, Upper Paleolithic, after Prideaux 1973: 130. <u>Bottom-center:</u> Mimbres B/w bowl motif, after Brody and others 1983: 89. <u>Bottom-right:</u> Mimbres B/w bowl, man-bird motif, which may depict Raven in both his human form and original white coloration (Feher-Elston 1991: 19-24; Luckert 1975:134-135), before he stole the sun to illuminate the earth and his feathers became sooty while flying through the smoke hole of the lodge of the sun's original owner. After Brody and others 1983: 112.

3—Icons Of The Hohokam Hamlets

Following the Archaic Period, East Central Arizona was dominated by two farming cultures, the Hohokam of the Salt River Valley, and the Mogollon of the Mogollon Rim. The Tonto Basin was largely influenced by the Hohokam, but the Globe-Miami Highlands tended toward the lifestyle of their Mogollon neighbors. About A.D. 750, population pressure in the Salt River Valley led to the movement of people up the Verde River, Tonto Creek, and the Gila and Salt River tributaries. The earliest evidence of Hohokam in the area, or at least one of their pots, was a few Snaketown Red-on-buff sherds Vickrey found during her excavation of Inspiration I (1945: 22-28).

The Globe-Miami Highlands settlements were small, scattered along streams where ditch irrigation of corn, beans, squash, and cotton was practical. Vickrey (1939), Gladwin (1957), and Crary, Germick, and Golio (1994) all comment on the lack of canals and other water control devices. Having owned a farm in the bottom of Kellner Canyon for over 60 years, we and our neighbors are aware of water control devices which are not apparent today. Three prehistoric reservoirs, one in upper Kellner Canyon, one at the junction of Kellner Canyon and upper Ice House Canyon, and one in upper Six Shooter Canyon, adjoined Gila Phase settlements, and were still in use by canyon residents in the 1950s. Although there are no large canals, remains of irrigation ditches still exist at the Brantley property upstream from Besh-Ba-Gowah. Hohokam sherds are few, but Hohokam three-quarter-grooved axes (some with ridges) are common enough as surface finds that the local farmers considered that the Hohokam dug a few ditches; the Salados expanded the area served by ditches, and lined some of them with stone; and in the early 1900s the Mormons, especially the Brantleys, cemented between the stones to prevent leakage (Jo Nell Brantley, personal communication, ca. 2005).

One reason for the apparent absence of irrigation devices is that before the area was deserted about A.D. 1440, the hillsides were so denuded of vegetation that adobe washed down the sides of the canyons covering the canyon-bottom fields. At the McKusick farm, six feet of rich black dirt is covered in places by a foot of adobe, making field farming impractical. Irrigation systems have been reported to the east at Talkalai Lake and along Gilson Wash, dating from the Gila Butte and Santa Cruz Phases (Crary, Germick, and Golio 1994: 58).

In addition to small scale ditch irrigation, the abundance of food which could be gathered must have been attractive. Hunting of animals was also possible, with species which inhabited the desert, the foothills, and the mountains close at hand.

The settlers lived in shallow pit houses, and used red-on-buff pottery and Hohokam three-quarter-grooved axes typical of the time. The northern section of Besh-Ba-Gowah was underlain by a scattering of shallow pit houses, some of which were excavated by Vickery, and a few excavated or re-excavated by Hohmann. The ridge which ran north-northwest from the north end of Gila Pueblo had six or eight shallow, oval pit houses scattered along each side of its crest. They were bladed away without excavation in the process of the construction of the college student parking lot.

Date (A.D.)	Period	Culture	Note
Present			
	Historic	San Carlos Apache & Yavapai*	ca.1890 Yavapai reoccupation of Gila Pueblo
1700			
	Proto-Historic	Yavapai	ca.1650 Yavapai reoccupation of Gila Pueblo
1450			
	Gila Phase	Salado	ca. 1440–1447 Final destruction of Gila Pueblo and Hagen site
1300			
	Roosevelt Phase	Salado	ca. 1225 Besh-Ba-Gowah and Gila Pueblo built
1200			
	Miami Phase	Mogollon-like Globe-Miami	Hohokam-like peoples move to San Carlos
1100			
	Sacaton Phase	Hohokam-like remnants	
1000			
	Santa Cruz Phase	Hohokam descendants	
850			
	Gila Butte Phase	Hohokam settlers	
800			
	Snaketown Phase	Hohokam settlers	
750			

Table 1. Formative Phase Sequence for the Globe-Miami Area.
(modified from Wood 1986: Figure 1; Crary, Germick, and Golio 1994: Table 1.)

*San Carlos Apache and Yavapai are of course separate cultures. In very early historic times Apaches occupied the south side of the Pinal Mountains. During the early to mid-1900s they lived in the canyon behind Bullion Plaza in Miami and at the junction of Russel Gulch and Pinal Creek, between Globe and Miami. According to the records of the Gila County Historical museum, the north side of the Pinal Mountains was occupied by the Stick-Standing-In-Water Yavapai Band. Yavapais lived in Wheatfield along Pinal Creek, just downstream from Globe, until they moved to Roosevelt, where they worked on the construction of Roosevelt Dam. After the completion of the dam, they moved to the Fort McDowell Indian Reservation.

Wood, McAllister, and Sullivan (1989: Figures 3, 4) include the Globe-Miami Highlands in the Hohokam Culture Area ca. A.D. 1000, and in the Salado Culture Area ca. A.D. 1300. Factors of geography, altitude, climate, and a limited but consistent water supply disqualified the upland settlements from participating in the Hohokam intensive canal irrigation network which was characterized by tight political control necessary to provide water to irrigate fields which lay miles from where it was taken from the river. There were no rivers in the Globe-Miami area, just small year-round streams watering canyon bottoms separated by high ridges.

Although the upland peoples were by necessity autonomous, during the Santa Cruz Phase they carried on practices and traditions characteristic of their Hohokam ancestors. Pottery was red-on-buff, manufactured by the paddle and anvil method, and decorated in the style of the day. Slate palettes, probably for mixing powdered pigments with medium for face and body paint, were in use, as were short, chunky cylindrical censers carved from soft volcanic rock. These iconic ceremonial artifacts (Figure 4), suggest a continuation of Hohokam religious practices of the period. In addition to already existing hunting shamanism and midwifery, Scarlet Macaws were imported into the Hohokam area at least as early as the A.D. 600s, indicating the veneration of Quetzalcoatl (Ka'yt-zal-co-atl), in his patronage of trade, engineering, and artificial water management (Figure 5) (McKusick 2001: 65-80; Phillips, VanPool and Vanpool 2006: 17-29; Thompson 2006: 165-183).

The Thick-billed Parrot, *Rhynchopsitta pachyrhyncha*, associated with Chalchihuitlicue (Chal-chee-we'et-lee-kway), also appears at Snaketown in the A.D. 600s. Her patronage of naturally occurring surface water was important to intensive irrigators, not only in providing supply, but also in preventing floods which are disastrous to communities whose survival depends upon efficient functioning of water control devices (McKusick 2001: 81-89; Miller and Taube 1993: 60; Burland and Forman 1975; 37-38, 93). By this time, her lunar personifications were being pictured in Mesoamerica (Figures 5 and 6).

Tightly controlled Hohokam social organization is evidenced by large public works such as extensive canal systems, enormous platform mounds with elite structures on top, ball courts, and an exuberant trade network, specializing in shell. Of these diagnostics, the only large public work in the Globe-Miami area is a ball court at Cutter, between Globe and San Carlos.

In contrast to their Hohokam history, the principal trade pottery of the period was Mogollon Red. These highly polished bowls, with their rich red exterior and smudged black interiors are considered by many to be the earliest popular tradeware in the area.

As time went on, wood supplies became depleted, and most of the Hohokam remnants moved on, apparently upstream, to continue their way of life in more productive drainages. The San Carlos area participated in this period of pit house villages, which continued on until the latest occupation of Gila Pueblo and Besh-Ba-Gowah as a supplier of San Carlos Red-on-Brown pottery. Presumably the Hohokam settlers cremated at least some of their dead, but the local folk, more Mogollon in custom, preferred inhumation.

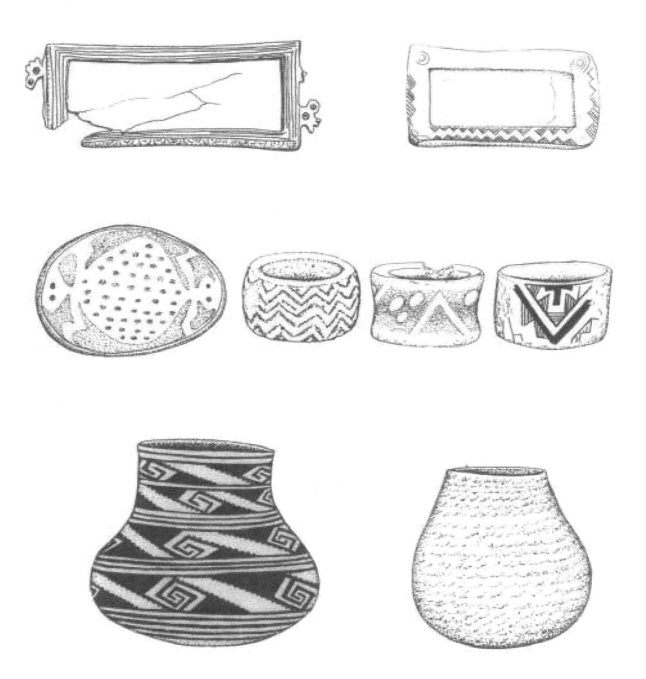

Figure 4. Palettes, Censers, and Burial Pottery. All sketched from Besh-Ba-Gowah displays. <u>Top</u>: Pinal schist palettes similar to Santa Cruz and Sacaton Phase palettes from Snaketown (compare Haury 1937: Plates CI, CV). <u>Middle-left</u>: Santa Cruz Red-on-buff double-horned-toad scoop, which may have solar retrograde and/or shamanic journey connotations. <u>Middle-right</u>: Santa Cruz Phase incised tuff censer, Santa Cruz Red-on-buff censer, and much later Gila Polychrome censer, all with chevron motif. The Gila Polychrome censer also has a Tau Cross motif. <u>Bottom</u>: preferred Salado burial pottery: left, San Carlos Red-on-brown, and right, Salado Red.

The sparse Mogollon-like population, which inhabited the uplands after the Hohokam-like people moved east, began to produce Salado Red, characterized by jars and deep hemispherical bowls thickly slipped with a raspberry red over the exterior, which may have fine indented corrugated texturing, and black smudged interiors. This came to be one of two preferred burial offerings. The other was vessels of San Carlos Red-on-brown, made of fine silty clay with a black smudged interior, and an exterior painted with Hohokam-derived designs.

William Underwood, who excavated over a thousand burials in sites ranging from La Ciudad de los Alamos/Armer Ranch Ruin, to Globe-Miami, to Dripping Springs, encompassing a very long time period reported this preference of burial wares extended from pre-Salado Polychrome times to the very end of the Salado occupation. Vickrey's room notes indicated that sherds found in rooms at various time periods reflected the popularity of different trade and locally produced wares through time, but her burial notes confirm Underwood's observations on the continuity of the preferred burial offerings despite changes in wares in daily use (Figure 4) (compare Wood 1987: 34, 40, 41).

Figure 5. Quetzalcoatl as Trade Patron Icon and Chalchihuitlicue Water Icons. L̲e̲f̲t̲: this avatar is identified by the Huastec cap; however, the buccal mask and wind jewel shell pectoral of Ehecatl are also shown, after Codex Telleriano-Remensisn, 16th Century Aztec, after Warren and Ferguson 1987: 4. C̲e̲n̲t̲e̲r̲: Chalchihuitlicue depicted in her whirlpool aspect on an Aztec feather disc (Burland and Forman 1975:93). R̲i̲g̲h̲t̲: Chalchihuitlicue, with turquoise cloud terrace nose ornament, pouring water on a corn plant, after Miller and Taube 1993: 61.

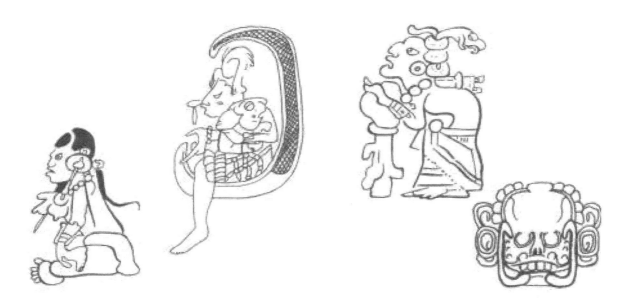

Figure 6. Lunar Icons. Left to right: maiden of the new moon; Matron of the full moon with rabbit, sitting in her dark, watery cave; crone of the waning moon with the serpent of wisdom in her hair (an alternate hair ornament is the spindle); skull with crescent moon jaws signifying the dark of the moon. Maiden and Crone after Dresden Codex, Coe 1975: 15. Matron, Late Classic incised vase, after Miller and Taube 1993: 119. Skull, Stela D, Quirigua, Late Classic, after Stone and Zender 2011: 146.

Figure 7. Rattlesnake Icons. <u>Top</u>: Mimbres B/w bowl design depicting a rattlesnake with four young; all bear the "hour glass" icon, after Brody 1977: 88. <u>Right</u>: Mimbres B/w bowl design showing traditional combat between rattlesnake and roadrunner, illustrating sky and earth complementary duality, with shamanic relevance, after Brody 1977: 210. <u>Bottom</u>: Cliff Polychrome bowl exterior painted with a rattlesnake face, from Kinishba, after Crown 1994: 153. Compare with the wristband in the lower-right of Figure 29.

4—Icons of the Upland Salado Pueblos

Power Bird and Animal Icons

Power birds and animals are generally large predators at the top of the food chain. The Holarctic Golden Eagle *Aquila chrysaetos*, is an example. In Mesoamerica, the Jaguar, *Felis onca,* is a revered power animal. It is replaced in the Southwest Culture Area by the Mountain Lion, *Felis concolor*, and the Black Bear, *Ursus americanus*. The patronage of a power animal is a common goal of the vision quest. Power animals often appear as icons depicted in natural form; as skin patterns, such as the jaguar's roseate markings; or as tracks, such as bear or mountain lion tracks Such "property qualifiers" are discussed in Stone and Zender (2011: 13-15.) Some less conspicuous animals are important because of mythical association. Deer represents the sun; rabbit represents the moon; and turtle represents the earth. Many of these creatures important in the Southwest are represented by glyphs in the Postclassic Mesoamerican day sign list, such as serpent, deer, rabbit, dog, jaguar, vulture, and eagle (Boone and Smith 2003: 189, Figure 24.6).

Shamanic Insects, Amphibians, Reptiles, Birds, and Mammals

Shamanic animals are different in some magical-appearing way from other living things. For example: they may be poisonous; they may hibernate; they may undergo unusual physical changes; they may leave unusual tracks; they may eat their own body parts; they may exhibit unusual powers of movement; they may reproduce in an unconventional manner; they may appear suddenly in large numbers, apparently from nowhere, and as suddenly be gone; or they may mimic human speech (Clara Lee Tanner, personal communication, 1952).

Centipedes

Centipedes are associated with night, water, and Chalchihuitlicue. A centipede is pictured in Figure 24, and in Figure 35, beaker design, lower-left. Centipedes are a favorite food of the Ringtail, (Bassariscus astutus), which lives adjacent to surface water, and appears in kiva paintings. Smith (1952: 202-225), presents an exhaustive discussion of most of the species listed herein.

Snakes

VanPool and VanPool (2007: 85-96) have identified a number of birds and animals depicted on Casas Grandes pottery which appear in shamanic contexts. Realistic depictions included the poisonous Western Coral Snake, *Micuroides euryxanthus*, and the Western Diamondback Rattlesnake, *Crotalus atrox*, along with the non-poisonous Sonoran Mountain King Snake, *Lampropeltis pyromelana*, and New Mexico Milk Snake *Lampropeltis triganulum celaenops*. While some snakes depicted are identifiable, others are generalized. Snakes appear in pairs of differing species, illustrating the concept of duality and/or twinning. The VanPools point out that snakes, which shed their skins, are associated with the earth, with rebirth, and with transformation. Because of their resemblance to lightning in their mode of movement and in their speed of strike, they are also associated with the sky, rain, and with the flight of projectiles which is a metaphor for impregnation and thus fertility, as well as for war.

Realistic depictions of rattlesnakes appear on Mimbres bowls, and on a Tonto Polychrome jar (Figure 7). The same rattlesnake "hourglass" icon is apparent in both pottery types, even though they are separated in time by at least 300 years (compare with the armband in Figure 29).

Feathered and/or Horned Serpents

The feathered and/or horned serpent is prominent in the study of Mesoamerican and Southwestern iconography. Phillips, VanPool, and VanPool (2006: 17-29) recognize the iconography of an organized horned serpent cult in the Mimbres Classic phase by ca. A.D. 1000, and subsequently on Salado Polychrome pottery. They further separate this movement at ca. A.D. 1300 into a cult identifiable by a forward-curving horn in Medio period Casa Grandes and in Jornada Mogollon art; and another cult identifiable by a backward curving horn, in Salado art.

The concept of the feathered and/or horned serpent as one entity presents a paradox. The feathered serpent/Quetzalcoatl association implies a sky function. The horned water serpent/Tlaloc association implies a subterranean water source function. On the surface these concepts appear to be mutually exclusive. From an ethnobiological point of view, serpent icons have three completely different origins in the natural world.

The oldest, most basic concept, which developed through time into the avatars of Quetzalcoatl, is the planet Venus as the Morning Star and Evening Star twins (Burland and Forman 1975:35). Ce Àcatl, the Morning Star Warrior, chased the stars from the sky so the sun could come up. Xolotl, the monstrous Evening Star twin, conducted the setting sun into the underworld. As Ce Àcatl is concerned with fertility, Xolotl is concerned with shamanic journeys, with resurrection, and with genetically doubled domestic crops (Crosswhite 1985: 114-116). The Horned Caterpillar, *Manduca sexta*, associated in Mimbres art with the sun-going-down concept, is the prototype for the forward-curving horned serpent (Figure 8). Hawk Moths may lay their eggs on various medicinal plants such as Mountain Evening Primrose, *Oenothera hookeri*, or Devil's Claw *Martynia* sp., but are most often associated with Datura, *Datura wrightii* which is treated in detail under psychoactive substances, below.

The head end of a horned caterpillar is inconspicuous and harmless, used mainly for eating enormous quantities of leaves. The tail end is quite different, consisting of two pseudopods and a horny scute which is dug into a plant stem to support the heavy caterpillar while it feeds. This grasping organ is very strong, and is capable of administering a painful and lasting pinch equivalent to being tweaked by a large gander. After a trip in March of 2011 to the Sierra Madre Occidental to visit a Tarahumara *curandera*, during which I was introduced to the shamanic use of the *gusano de pica*, the "caterpillar which pinches," I spent the following summer encouraging the growth and development of horned caterpillars. To observe them preparing themselves for their descent into the earth to pupate, I spent entire mornings sitting motionless on a box in the blazing sun. Once a caterpillar achieves maximum corpulence, it

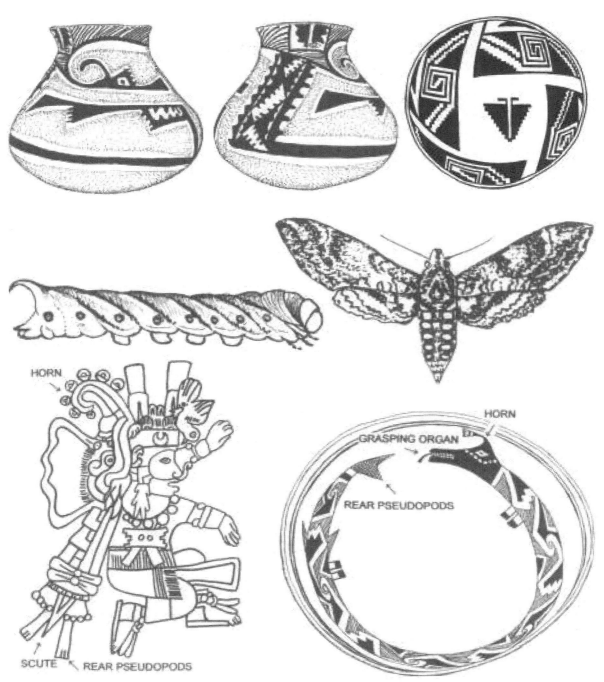

Figure 8. Horned Caterpillar Icons. <u>Top-left and center</u>: two views of an unprovenienced local Tonto Polychrome canteen jar painted with naturalistic horned caterpillar and Hawk Moth, on display at the Bullion Plaza Museum, Miami, Arizona. <u>Top-right</u>: Gila Polychrome bowl, from Besh-Ba-Gowah, with a Hawk Moth at its center. The gap between the wings is a "spirit path." (Taube 2010:115–118). Not to scale relative to the jar views to the left. <u>Center</u>: a horn worm and Hawk Moth. <u>Bottom-left</u>: Xiutecutli, Lord of Fire, with turquoise "butterfly" pectoral and "fire serpent" back piece, displaying horn, scute, and rear pseudopods, Codex Borbonicus, after Brundage 1979: 23. <u>Bottom-right</u>: Mimbres B/w bowl showing tasseled horn, grasping organ as mouth, and "fishtail" appearance of the rear pseudopods after the scute has been eaten off; after Brody 1977: 197.

descends from the plant upon which it is feeding and rests on the slender stem of a Nightshade, *Solanum elaegnifolium,* which bends over with the weight to just above the ground. At this stage the caterpillar is covered with a loose, translucent, pea green, outer skin. The caterpillar's beautiful black and white markings and eye-spots are no longer visible. The caterpillar releases the stem except for the two rear pseudopods, walks down the right side of its own body with its true legs, and begins chewing away its scute. Then, it walks back up itself and down the left side of its body, and finishes devouring the horny scute, leaving only a ragged, straw-colored circle of bare flesh below its horn and above its rear pseudopods. The caterpillar immediately tumbles to the earth, and sets off at about a foot a minute searching for a secure log or rock to burrow under. The two rear pseudopods now look like the tail of a fish, as they push strongly to propel the caterpillar into the earth. Apparently it is necessary for the caterpillar to eat the scute off so that it is detached from its old outer skin, and can assume its pupa form. Eventually, the pupa hatches and emerges from the earth as a Hawk Moth, an icon for rebirth. The process of the horned caterpillar eating off its scute may well be the model for the Old World Worm Oroboros motif which illustrates a serpent eating its tail, and is also an icon for rebirth.

VanPool and VanPool (2007: 75, Figure 5.4) picture a Casas Grandes pottery design featuring a horn worm with prominent rear eye spots, horn, two rear pseudopods, and a forked tongue where the pain-inflicting scute would be. Feathers springing from the base of the horn may refer to shamanic flight induced by datura intoxication.

The Hawk Moth icon appears on a Gila Polychrome bowl from Besh-Ba-Gowah centered between offset quarters, suggesting an association at this site with Xiuhtecutli, "he who was, is, and will be," who was the patron of the directions, time, and the hearth. An excellent illustration of the structure of the horn worm appears in an Aztec codex showing Xiutecutli (Shee-uh-tee-coot-lee), with a "fire serpent" backpiece (Figure 8). An unprovenienced local Tonto Polychrome canteen jar is painted on each side with a horn worm on a stem and a Hawk Moth near the rim. These creatures are painted realistically in heavy black line, as was the style in vogue in the mid-A.D. 1400s. If the pinching end of the caterpillar is rendered as a fictional mouth, as it was on Mimbres black-on-white bowls, the horn is perceived as pointing forward, not back as it should be in the Salado generalization. The reason for this apparent contradiction is that the Horned Serpent is a representation of a caterpillar and the Feathered Serpent is a representation of another creature (Storer 1943:593).

The second horned serpent icon appears earliest as an ancient Maya duck god depiction of the Ehecatl avatar of Quetzalcoatl. In his beneficent guise, Ehecatl blows the rain clouds from the mountains where they are formed, to rain upon the fields. In his destructive guise, Ehecatl is the whirl wind. Paired duck gods are depicted by the Maya as duck-masked Venus hero twins, marked with *IK'* (wind) and *POLAW* (ocean) hieroglyphs painted on their bodies (Stone and Zender 2011: 45, 175). The biological source for this icon is the Muscovy duck, *Cairina moschata,* the head of which appears as the Aztec day sign for Ehecatl, Wind (Figure 9). The Muscovy duck is peculiar in that it does not quack like other ducks; it hisses. Its red, featherless face is the source for the red coloration of the Ehecatl buccal mask. Sexual dimorphism is extreme. The very large males are extremely aggressive and may fight to the death during the breeding season. One of my drakes successfully defended himself from attack by a hungry, two hundred pound black bear by repeatedly flying in its face and beating it with his strong wings. Another unusual feature of the Muscovy drake is its copulatory organ, which is corkscrew-shaped and over eight inches long (Mone 2012: 72).

Figure 9. Duck God and Water Dog Icons. <u>Top-left</u>: Maya Muscovy-Duck-headed gods with left, POLAW ocean/sea, and right IK' wind/breath, markings on arm, back, and thigh; after Stone and Zender 2011: 174. <u>Top-right</u>: male Muscovy duck head with red, unfeathered face, after Austin 1961: 68. Lower-right: day sign icon for Ehecatl, "wind," after Vaillant 1951: 191. <u>Middle-left</u>: water dog, larval form of Tiger Salamander, *Ambystoma tigrinum*. <u>Bottom-left</u>: Tiger Salamander, adult form. The water dog serves as the model for the feathered serpent, and the Tiger Salamander bears the starry icon of the Milky Way, after Storer 1943: 593.

The third icon depicts a water/feather association. The water dog or *axtolotl* is the larval form of the Tiger Salamander A*mbystoma tigrinum*. The larval form has a fringe of feather-like external gills, giving rise to the "feathered serpent" motif. The adult form is black with creamy-white spots, duplicating the Milky Way icon. The water dog is unusual in that it may reproduce in the larval feather-gilled form, rather than develop into a Tiger Salamander. I believe this is the original model for the Feathered Serpent (Figure 9).

Frogs, Turtles, and Lizards

A Gila Polychrome bowl recovered from the excavation of Besh-Ba-Gowah bears a design which is a composite of frog, turtle, and Horned Lizard characteristics (Figure 10). Frogs are unusual in that they transform from tadpoles into adults. They also hibernate, as do turtles and lizards. Turtle shells were, and are still, made into ceremonial rattles. This creation is seen by many groups as resting on the back of a great turtle. Sonoran Mud Turtle, *Kinosternon sonoriense* shell was recovered from both Besh-Ba-Gowah and Gila Pueblo. This aquatic species is found in forested areas above 1,550 m. The same turtle species was found in the water system at Paquimé, despite the fact that it is located in a low altitude cholla forest. This turtle is apparently a deliberate and symbolic import (VanPool and VanPool 2007: 29).

Local children are instructed not to bother Horned Lizards because they "shoot blood from their eyes." Horned Lizards are extremely unusual in that they defend themselves by spraying a perceived attacker from head to toe with a fine red mist, after which they fall inert. When the attacker is gone, they revive and go their way. Desert Horned Lizard, *Phrynosoma platyrhinos*, bone was recovered from Besh-Ba-Gowah.

The Western Skink, although it is a lizard, appears to be a snake with a pair of hind legs. The Many-lined Skink, *Eumeces multivirigatus*, is still common in the Globe foothills. A two-legged skink is depicted on a Gila Polychrome bowl found at Besh-Ba-Gowah (Figure 10).

Figure 10. Frog, Turtle, and Lizard Icons. Gila Polychrome bowl designs from Besh-Ba-Gowah depicting, left, a skink; and right, a composite frog-turtle-horned lizard.

Zygodactylous Birds

Zygodactylous birds are hatched with the first pedal digit, analogous to a big toe, directed backwards, and the second, third, and fourth pedal digits directed forward like other birds. Shortly after hatching, the outer, fourth pedal digit swivels to the rear, giving an X-shaped foot and track. Zygodactylous birds include parrots, woodpeckers, trogons, and roadrunners. The feathers of all are important in ritual. The X-shaped track of the roadrunner is used in art to symbolize the shamanic journey, because it is the same going out and coming back (Clara Lee Tanner, personal communication 1952). Shamanic practitioners always emphasize that the student must never journey to a place they do not know how to get back from, and that the student must always come back exactly the way they went out. The VanPools (2007: 75, Figure 5.4) illustrate a zygodactylous roadrunner pottery design.

Shamanic practitioners work with an assistant who protects their person from distractions, disruptions, or harm during a shamanic journey. If the shaman should fail to return as promptly as they should, the assistant is responsible for talking them home. The shamanic Venus hero twin, Xolotl (Sho-lottle), is depicted with at least one foot, if not both feet and both hands, on backwards, as an indication of the retrograde motion of the sun during its nocturnal journey through the underworld. The foot-on-backward Xolotl icon is illustrated in Figure 11.

Figure 11. Foot-on-backward Xolotl Icons. <u>Top</u>: Xolotl depicted with two Venus stars, pendant eyeball, and backward hands and feet, symbolizing the retrograde motion of the sun in the underworld, simplified from Miller and Taube 1993: 191. <u>Right</u>: entranced Casas Grandes shamanic figure with # "ladder/ascent" signs and one foot on backward, after VanPool and VanPool 2007: 75. <u>Bottom</u>: shaman curing, with one foot on backward, Mimbres B/w, after Brody 1977: 50.

Bird Icons Associated with the Monsoon Season

A swallow is depicted in a Gila Polychrome bowl recovered from Besh-Ba-Gowah. Swallows are also depicted on Mimbres B/w bowls. Violet Green Swallows, *Tachycineta thalassina,* breed locally, but are only seen following monsoon rains when they fly in groups of twenty or so, back and forth in the mist, catching insects (Figure 12).

Poorwills, *Phalaenoptilus nuttallii,* live in the Globe-Miami area year-round and are unusual in that they hibernate briefly during the extreme cold before and after the winter solstice when their insect food is not available. Hibernation is a death and resurrection theme which is associated with shamanic trance. Poorwills call after sundown for a night or two before a rain.

In Pima mythology, Poorwills were instrumental in the fall of the southern Big Houses. The residents of these pueblo-like structures were called the Vipishad. They were a small pueblo people like the Hopi. A taller people, called the Vupshkam, were said to have emerged from the underworld, marching from the east or south, conquering and destroying the Big Houses and their occupants as they encountered them along the middle Gila River and the lower Salt River. When the inhabitants of a Big House were successful in defending themselves, the Vupshkam sent shamans, who had the power to appear as certain animals, to make the Vipishad helpless. A version of this conquest story was recorded by Julian D. Hayden in 1935 at Snaketown on the Gila River Indian Reservation, south of Phoenix. In this case, a bird called *koologam,* or Poorwill, was sent because of the birds' habit of hibernating during the winter months, when there were no insects for them to eat. Influenced by this Poorwill shaman, the Vipishad lost their strength, happily lay down to sleep, and were overcome. The Pima elders born around 1910 were still able to point out locations where these events were supposed to have occurred. These elders considered that the Vupshkam were now the Pima (Rea 2007a: 189; 2007b).

Poorwills feed in huge swirling flocks of untold thousands at sunset during the monsoon season. Robert and I have driven for about 20 miles through the lower San Pedro River Valley from Mammoth to Winkelman, Arizona, without ever reaching a break in the feeding Poorwills wheeling over our heads. The Santa Cruz Phase Hohokam of the A.D. 800s depicted this phenomenon in their red on buff pottery designs, with stylized bird motifs spiraling clockwise from the center to the margin of flaring bowls (Figure 12). An enormous flaring feasting bowl with this design rendered in Gila Polychrome was smashed as part of the site-closing ceremonies following the destruction of Gila Pueblo in the mid-A.D.-1400s.

Figure 12. Bird Icons of the Monsoon Season. <u>Left</u>: Swallow, Gila Polychrome bowl design, Besh-Ba-Gowah. <u>Center</u>: Poorwill, Mimbres Polychrome bowl design, after Brody and others 1983: 99. <u>Right</u>: mid-1400s rendition of Santa Cruz Red-on-buff swirling Poorwill design rendered on an enormous flaring Gila Polychrome feasting bowl, from Gila Pueblo (compare Haury 1976: Fig. 12.97).

Hummingbirds as War and Resurrection Icons

Hummingbirds were seen as war icons simply because they seem to fight over just about everything: they fight over the twigs on which they sit to catch insects. They fight over mates. They attack creatures many times their size. Among the Mesoamericans, they are associated with bloodletting, as are the tubular flowers from which they sip nectar. Upon death, warriors and women who die in childbirth are transported to the most glorious heaven, where they become hummingbirds and hover around the sun. Huitzilopochtli, "Hummingbird on the Left," the southern Tezcatlipoca, who was the patron of the Aztecs, is often shown with a long-beaked hummingbird mask (Miller and Taube 1993 98).

The resurrection imagery connected with hummingbirds probably derives from the fact that all hummingbirds at this altitude fly south for the winter except male Anna's Hummingbirds, *Calypte anna*. At sunset, these males fall into torpor, which lowers their metabolism enough for them to survive the winter nights. At sunrise, they awaken, and resume their hunt for food. Their awakening is controlled by the light of the sun, not by the heat of the sun. Another unusual feature is that males of this species sing when perched.

Hummingbirds are common motifs on Mimbres black-on-white bowls, I am not aware of the recovery of any tiny hummingbird bones from a southwestern site, but I identified a tassel made from the entire tail of a female Broad-tailed Hummingbird, *Selasphorus platycercus*, recovered from the excavation of Inscription House in northern Arizona. It is a good match to the tassel dangling from the headdress in Figures 13 and 30.

Icons of the Night

According to the VanPools (2007: 105), the Tarahumara Indians report hearing a spirit bird at night that calls "Sht! Sht!" Kathleen Condit reports that female bronzed cowbirds, *Tangavius aeneus*, produce this nocturnal call. Females of this species lay their eggs in the nests of other birds, to the detriment of the original inhabitants.

The barn owl, *Tyto alba,* is identified from the head of a fragmentary bird jar recovered during the excavation of Besh-Ba-Gowah. It was originally part of a jar with a horizontal axis, like other local jars which have heads reminiscent of quail (Figure 13). Barn owl and horned owl hooded effigy jars from Casas Grandes have a vertical axis. Owls are still highly regarded at Zuni, in contrast to many other modern pueblos (VanPool and VanPool 2007: 103-104).

Bats, particularly the little brown bat, *Myotis lucifugus*, may be seen in the last light on summer evenings. Giant bats are considered obstacles for both the sun and the departed on their journey into the underworld. A bat-costumed man is depicted with a complex headdress on a Mimbres B/w bowl painted in the early A.D. 1100s. Two high-status males who were killed during the final attack at Gila Pueblo in the A.D. 1440s, were wearing the same headdresses (Figure 13). The bat-costumed man is interpreted by some as a shaman, but both of his feet are in the usual position. The evidence gained from the Gila Pueblo excavation suggests that these personages served primarily as moiety leaders, and only secondarily as shamans.

Figure 13. Icons of the Night. <u>Top</u>: barn owl and two views of barn owl effigy jar, Tonto Polychrome, Besh-Ba-Gowah. <u>Bottom-left</u>: masked personator costumed as a bat, Mimbres Polychrome bowl design, after Brody and others 1983: Figure 6. The bat wings are decorated with the Milky Way design. <u>Bottom-right</u>: White-tailed Deer with tie-dye Milky Way design, Mimbres bowl design, Treasure Hill, after Davis, 1995:131.

Venus Icons

Venus, the third most brilliant object in the night sky, one which can cast a shadow, is viewed as twins. In art, the morning star aspect is rendered as lighter in color, and the evening star aspect as darker in color, as in Figure 14 (Crown 1994: Figures 5.28 and 9.1; Thompson 2006: 172-177). If personified, the elder, Ce Àcatl, morning star twin is identifiable by parallel lines of face paint on the cheek (Brody and others 1983: 115, 118-119, 121-123), by a missing arm, or by being a victim of sacrifice. The younger, Xolotl, evening star twin, is depicted in the role of sacrificer and shaman-resuscitator. Morning and evening stars are usually indicated in Salado ceramic design as equal-armed crosses, like plus signs. The Maya *EK'* sign, for star/planet/constellation, precedes the Salado Venus icon (Stone and Zender 2011: 150-151).

Quail, which vocalize at sunrise and sunset, may be painted with the four-point star of morning, the four-petal mountain evening primrose blossom of sunset, or the Milky Way design of night (Figure 39).

Venus may also be painted as a star with many points. A male human effigy jar recovered from a ceremonial room at Gila Pueblo was painted with a medicine pouch on the right hip decorated with a star with multiple points. His back was painted with a half-cloud terrace blanket design associated with Tlaloc (Figure 29).

Figure 14. Venus Twin Icons. Top left: Maya EK', star/planet/constellation, after Stone and Zender 2011: 150-151. Top-center: Mimbres star, after Brody 1977: 71; "morning star," "evening star," after Thompson 2006: 175. Top-right: Salado star, "morning star" and "evening star," after Crown 1994: Figures 5.28 and 9.1. Center: younger brother left, elder brother right under the blanket of night depicting sunset, Milky Way, and sunrise, centered in a Venus cross, after Brody and others 1983: 122. Bottom-left: younger brother wearing horn worm costume, sacrificing elder brother, after Davis 1995: 180. Bottom-right: twins with warrior caps carried on a basket holding "morning star" and "evening star," after Davis 1995: 157.

Tlaloc Icons

Tlaloc, the patron of thunder, lightning, and rain, is depicted in the Southwest as a goggle-eyed, burial bundle wrapped in a cloud-step patterned blanket. The cloud-step in half, single, and double versions, is a favorite decoration on Salado pottery (Figures 15, 21, and 22).

Otherworldly Place Icons

At Besh-Ba-Gowah, the Tau cross, "**T**", decorates a censer (Figure 4). Another may be painted on a beaker-shaped jar from the "twin" burial excavated by Vickrey (Figure 16). The interred children were 6-7 year olds, both of whom had died violently from a blow with a small object which penetrated their skulls above the left eye socket. Shooting in the back with arrows and skull smashing appear to be the most common causes of violent death among the Upland Salado. The Tau cross appears earlier as the Maya IK' sign, for wind/breath. When the *IK'* wind sign is combined with the *WITZ mountain* sign, they characterize an otherworldly location. The Tau cross appears elsewhere in the Southwest as T-shaped doorways in Chaco Canyon and at Paquimé (Stone and Zender 2011: 107, 174-175).

The VanPools (2007: 74-75) illustrate Casas Grandes pottery designs depicting entranced shaman marked with pound signs, #. One of the Maya signs for *EHB*, step, is a lashed ladder section in pound sign form. The connotation of this sign is "to ascend," a reasonable activity for an entranced shaman on his way the Unseen Universe (Figure 16).

Figure 15. Goggle-eyed Tlaloc Icons. <u>Top-left</u>: Mimbres B/w bowl design, early A.D. 1100s, after Davis 1995: 171. <u>Top-center</u>: Jornada Mogollon petroglyph, A.D. 1050-1400, after Schaafsma 1994 and 2000: 65. <u>Top-right</u>: Tonto Polychrome jar neck design, A.D. 1350-1450, after Crown 1994: 157. <u>Bottom-left</u>: pictograph, Picture Cave, Hueco area, West Texas. <u>Bottom-right</u>: pictograph in cave on west side of Alamo Hueco Mountains, southwest New Mexico, both after Cosgrove 1947: Figures 45 and 46.

Figure 16. Otherworldly Place Icons. <u>Left</u>: EHB, Maya wooden ladder step glyph, connoting ascension, after Stone and Zender 2011: 107. <u>Center</u>: Tonto Polychrome jar decorated with Tau cross, from burial of two children at Besh-Ba-Gowah, A.D. 1350-1450, sketched from Vickrey's field photo. <u>Right</u>: Maya IK' wind/breath glyph surmounted by WITZ mountain glyph, signifying otherworldly place, after Stone and Zender 2011: 174-175.

5—Psychoactive Substances Used by Followers of Late Pre-Hispanic Mesoamerican God Cults

Mesoamerican God Cults and Birds of Sacrifice

Young (1994 and 2000: 107-120) provides an excellent summary of Historic Pueblo and Mesoamerican correspondences. Pre-Hispanic Mesoamerican God Cults are present in the Southwest about 300 B.C., along with the Uto-Aztecan language, new maize cultivars, and the Small Indian Domestic Turkey phenotype. The easiest way to trace and date these cults is by following the occurrences of sacrificial birds (McKusick 2001: 17-18).

Xiuhtecutli Cult

The earliest of these supernaturals, identified by raven sacrifice, was the Old World Raven, the eternal shape-changer, who evolved in North America into the "center place" identified as "Polaris," the ruler of the four quarters of the earth, who lived in the heart of the volcano, and in the pueblo home was honored by a central hearth (Compare Xiuhtecutli's hawk moth centered between four quadrants on the bowl in Figure 8) (DiPeso 1974: 556-558; Brundage 1979: 1-5,15,22; Coe 1975:24; Luckert 1975:178-179, 220). He and his wife came with the Paleo-Indian Hunters, and remained with the Archaic Peoples. With the Mesoamerican transition from hunting and gathering to farming, he changed his form to that of Huehueteotl (Way-way-ta'y-otl), the Old Fire God, a hunch-backed old man bearing a censer on his shoulders. By Aztec times he was known as Xiuhtecutli (Shee-oo-te-co'otli), Lord of Fire, who dwells in the heart of the volcano. As creator, "He Who Was, Is, and Shall Be," he is present at all time levels (McKusick 2001: 25-37).

Tlaloc Cult

Tlaloc (Tla'h-loc), a god of underground water sources and rain, is traced in the greater North American Southwest by the head-and-neck sacrifice of the Small Indian Domestic Turkey (Di Peso 1974: 565–569; McKusick 1986: p. 4, and Figures 16 and 17; McKusick 20001: pp. 40-45, Figures 17 and 18) and at Paquimé by turkey and child sacrifice. Western Pueblo legends tell of sacrificing a little boy and a little girl to Tlaloc to stop a drought. Tlaloc resides underground and in mountain top caves, and generates rain clouds which are necessary for successful farming. He is often depicted as a burial bundle wrapped in a cloud-step-design blanket. The earliest maize in the Southwest dates to about 2100 B.C., and the earliest canals date to about 1500 B.C. (Herr 2009: 1; Roney and Hard 2009: 3-4). Maize growing spread rapidly and there is no apparent single route of introduction. Maize was first grown to supplement gathered foods, and not until about 300 B.C. do we see the first sign of Tlaloc worship appear along with the introduction of the Small Indian Domestic Turkey, *Meleagris gallopavo "tularosa."* This phenotype was small, hump-backed, and dark-plumaged, with feathers extending up its neck all the way to the head. Osteological remains demonstrate that it was brought, along with a new strain of maize, into southwestern New Mexico, moved north just east of the Arizona-New Mexico boundary, and arrived in the Four Corners area before 100 B.C. (McKusick 2001: 39-49; compare Bullock 2007: 6).

Chalchihuitlicue Cult

Tlaloc has a beautiful, adolescent sister or consort, Chalchihuitlicue (Chal-chee-we'et-lee-kway), Our Lady Precious Green, She of the Turquoise Skirt. She is the goddess of naturally flowing water on the surface of the ground: springs, streams, rivers, and lakes. In her dark-of-the-moon manifestation, she is the whirlpool or even the flood (Miller and Taube: 2007: 60, 61,184; McKusick 2001: 81-89). Southern Arizona legends relate the practice of sacrificing a little girl and a little boy to stop flooding (Frank Crosswhite, personal communication, about 1985).

Chalchihuitlicue is a patroness of birth, baptism, and corn in the milk stage. She is a powerful fertility figure, impregnated by a dart thrust from Ce Àcatl, the Venus as Morning Star Warrior avatar of Quetzalcoatl (Figure 37). Chalchihuitlicue is traced by the amniotic fluid/string apron (Figure 1), and the rabbit in the moon icons (Figure 6). Her introduction in Mesoamerican form is marked by burials of Military Macaws, totaling 81, and Thick-billed Parrots, totaling 15, in the Southwest proper and Paquimé combined. They extend in time from the A.D. 600s to 1450 (McKusick 1974: 285; McKusick 1976: 374-377, McKusick 2001: 88). Other indicators are deposits of green stone. A green stone axe effigy was used in the closing ceremony of Kiva 1, AZ W:10:37 (ASM), a Tularosa Phase site at Point of Pines. A bowling-ball-sized greenstone manuport, and another greenstone axe, were found during the excavation of the ca. A.D. 1440 level of the ceremonial/redistribution complex at Gila Pueblo. A sacred baseball-sized green stone, representing half of the Earthmother's heart, still rests nested in eagle feathers in a deerskin bag, lashed into a basket kept by O'odam ceremonialists at Quitobac (McKusick 2001: 81-89).

Quetzalcoatl Cult

Quetzalcoatl (Ka'yt-zal-co-atl), the Plumed Serpent, is a complex supernatural with a great many avatars. As Tlaloc is god of water, both underground and in the sky, and Chalchihuitlicue is goddess of water flowing naturally on the ground, Quetzalcoatl is god of water in ditches, canals, pipes, aqueducts, and reservoirs. He is the patron of engineering, education, arts, crafts, trade, music, and the finer things of civilization (DiPeso 1974: 548-555: Miller and Taube 1993: 141-142,166; Young 1994-2000: 113-115; Burland and Forman 1975: 49).

As Ce Àcatl (Say A'h-catl), Venus as the Morning Star Warrior/Elder Brother, he chases the stars out of the sky so the sun can come up. He is a fertility god, impregnating Chalchihuitlicue by striking her with his dart (McKusick 2001: 83, 85). He is a god of spring, and may be traced in the Southwest from the A.D. 600s to 1450 by the remains of Scarlet Macaws sacrificed and buried at the Spring Equinox (McKusick 20001: 72, 74). Scarlet Macaw feathers are still essential to pueblo worship.

As Xolotl (Sho'-lottle), Venus as the Evening Star/Younger Brother, he brings the sun down into the underworld. He is depicted as a monstrous deformed being with dog-like features. His feet are on backwards, indicating the retrograde motion of the sun as it travels through the underworld. He is a resurrection figure, signifying return from the dead, and as such is patron of the shaman. He is also the patron of domestic plants involving monstrous genetic doubling, such as domestic maguey and maize (Burland and Forman 1975:35-37; Miller and Taube, 190-191; Crosswhite 1985: 114-115).

As Ehecatl (Ay'-hay-catl), Lord of the Wind, he brings the clouds generated by Tlaloc to rain upon the fields. In his sinister manifestation, he is the whirlwind (DiPeso 1974: 548-550).

Sun Cults

The most constant attribute of the sun is its association with, and sacrifice of, the high-flying eagle. It is important as a Sky Father in complementary duality with the Earth Mother. Beyond that, it is submerged in complexity. In Mesoamerica, the sun took on a variety of tribal manifestations. To some, it dies at the end of each age and is born again at the beginning of the succeeding age, or even at the dawning of each day. This is derived from a Mesoamerican myth about a son who hunts quail, only to have the bones of his dead father turn into a deer, which springs away in a flash of light (Brundage 1979: 38).

To most pueblo people, the sun enters the land of the departed at sunset, lighting their day during the night hours of the world above, and emerges again into the middle world of living mankind at sunrise. Icons for the sun include sunflowers (Figures 19 and 40), deer, antelope, and quail (McKusick 2001: 50, 63).

Tezcatlipoca Cult

Tezcatlipoca (Tez-cat-li-po'-ca), The Smoking Mirror, is known early among the Maya as ruler of the surface of the earth. He tempted the Earth Monster, an enormous caiman, with his left foot. She bit off his foot, but he tore off her lower jaw, so she can no longer sink beneath the waters. Now all mankind lives upon her back. The ancient Mesoamericans saw him as Huitzilopochtli, the sun at the zenith, in the daytime. At night, Tezcatlipoca was the Big Dipper, hopping around the North Star on his one remaining foot, in opposition to Earth Monster who appears as the constellation Cassiopia. The shank and foot of the Large Indian Domestic Turkey is found as a sacrifice to Tezcatlipoca, as a replacement for his lost foot, in Mexico and in sites served by the Hohokam Trade Network (Bradley 1999: Figure 16.7; McKusick 2001: 91-94). In Mesoamerica he is associated with jaguar; in the Southwest, with mountain lion and bear.

Tezcatlipoca becomes a war god in time, specializing in ambush and nocturnal infiltration, and is associated with sorcery. On his breast he wears an obsidian mirror, into which he peers, like a crystal ball, to foretell the future. Turkey leg and foot sacrifices to Tezcatlipoca pertain almost entirely to the height of Chaco Canyon influence, about A.D.1000, and depictions of Tezcatlipoca in art pertain to Hohokam platform mound settlements. A late occurrence of foot and leg sacrifice was recovered from the Upper Ruin at Tonto National Monument which lies on the eastern margin of the Hohokam Trade Network. The Globe-Miami Upland Salado sites lie within the Casas Grandes Trade Network, where Tezcatlipoca as a war god is not discernable in either art or faunal remains (McKusick 2001: 91-97).

Xipe Totec Cult

The western, red, avatar of Tezcatlipoca is Xipe Totec (She'e-pay To'-tec), Our Lord the Flayed One, who appears in Mesoamerican art as an Aztec priest wearing the flayed skin of a sacrificial victim, and at Casas Grandes as human effigy pots with closed eyes and gaping mouths. Xipe Totec is associated with death, suffering, scalping, decapitation, trophy taking, dancing with human trophies, and with cannibalism (Di Peso 1974: 560-563).

Items of cultural diffusion, which enter a new area, are treated in several ways: they may be accepted, they may be changed, or they may be rejected. There is no evidence to date of cannibalism among the Upland Salado. However, there is evidence that the Tonto Basin Salado took human body part trophies, and that the Upland Salado were victims of trophy taking.

Ash Creek, AZ U:3:49 (ASU) is a small Gila Phase community lying on the west side of Tonto Creek, above the northern end of what is now Roosevelt Lake. It had seven masonry rooms, plus various outdoor roasting pits, ramadas, hearths, wing walls, a clay mixing pit, and trash middens. Hohmann, et al., report that among human remains recovered were 63 inhumations, one cremation, and ten individuals represented only by bundled body parts found on the floor of Room 3. It appears that long bones of various individuals, more often from the arms than from the legs, were hung from the structural beams of the roof or fastened to the wall on the west side of the room. The deaths of these ten individuals apparently occurred over an extended period of time. Included were two adult females, a juvenile female, "an extremely small statured adult male, a fifteen-year old individual who had probably lost the use of his left leg, a 16 to 19 year old individual, and four adults of unknown sex. Shortly after their death, these individuals were dismembered. Forceful manipulation of these limb bones occurred during dismemberment, reflected by the green bone spiral breakage." Some bundles were from one individual; some bundles contained bones from more than one individual. Perhaps each bundle represented body parts gathered during separate trophy taking episodes. Apparently the remains were dried, and then kept covered. There is no evidence of cannibalism or ancestor worship. The most probable explanation for these bundles is that they are the accumulated trophies of opportunistic attacks on helpless inhabitants of distant villages, who remained at home while their men folk were absent (Hohmann, Fortin, Howard, and O'Brien 1985: 242, 257-264).

Trophy taking, with the Upland Salado as victims, is demonstrated in the discovery, by William Underwood, of a skeleton at Pinal Pueblo which was missing its hands. Underwood reburied the bones in horror, and led me to the site. The victim was a tall, 5-foot 4-inch adult woman, who had been struck a ghastly, smashing blow to the back of her head, fracturing the occipital bone. Her hands had been removed, but she lay still alive on the ground for long enough for her wound to infect and erode the bone. Someone eventually dug a trench 18 inches deep just downhill from her body, which was pupating flesh flies, slid her into it, and covered her with a little earth.

It appears that Xipe Totec was directly relevant to the Tonto Basin Salado, in the Hohokam Trade Network, but was only indirectly relevant to the Upland Salados, who appear to have had serious problems with the Tonto Basin Salado from A.D. 1260 on. Triangular arrow points identical to those found at the Armer Ranch Site occur associated with the A.D. 1260 and

1440s destructions of Gila Pueblo, and of Bead Mountain (Figure 30) (McKusick and Young 1997: 54, 110, Figure 27 h; William Underwood, personal communication, 1972).

Mesoamerican Supernaturals and Psychoactive Substances

Emil W. Haury considered the Tarahumara to be a late remnant of mountain-adapted aboriginal culture, with probable similarities to that of the Upland Salado (personal communication, 1952). Therefore, in March of 2011, my husband Robert and I, and our daughter Kathleen Condit, traveled to the Barranca del Cobre, Chihuahua, Mexico, to visit Sra. Conchita Mancinas, a Tarahumara *curandera*. She was a tiny, youthful 75-year-old with sparkling eyes. She had worked for a lifetime with her recently deceased husband, and was then assisted by her granddaughter. At the time of our visit, she had 17 children, 54 grandchildren, and 27 great grandchildren. She was most proud of her practice as a midwife; and claimed she had attended 300 births without losing either a mother or a child. The purpose of our visit was to show her color copies of pictures mounted on 3 × 5 inch cards to see if local plants or motifs on Salado, Casas Grandes, and Mimbres pottery were meaningful to her. In addition to showing her the pictures, I asked four brief, non-leading questions:

> *¿Conoce este?* Are you acquainted with this?
> *¿Comolo llama?* How is it called?
> *¿Usa este?* Do you use it?
> *¿Para que?* What for?

The method worked well. Sra. Mancinas had an extensive collection of plants which were useful for treating most of the common afflictions of mankind. The great surprise was not how many plants local to the Globe-Miami Highlands are also used by the Tarahumara today, but how many of these plants, which are medicinal in small quantities, become psychoactive when taken in large quantities. Most remarkable of all was the idea of psychoactive substances being delivered in the form of ceremonial face and body paint. This technique would introduce a quick, small, dose of the desired medicinal into the blood stream of the patient through paracutaneous absorption. It would also alter their perception, relieving pain or other distress. A *curandera* who could deliver the proper prayers, blessings, or songs, and at the same time produce an actual analgesic effect, coupled with the perception of divine intervention, would be in great demand.

When I showed her a picture of a horn worm on a datura plant, she was delighted and exclaimed, "*¡Gusano que pica!*" "The caterpillar that pecks!"

At this point she grasped the forefinger of her left hand from the sides with the fore and middle fingers of her right hand, and dug the thumb nail of her right hand into the pad of her left forefinger, illustrating how the caterpillar uses its grasping organ to support its heavy body on a stem. The head end of the horn worm is harmless, equipped only for masticating enormous quantities of datura leaves, but the tail end is something else again. The grasping organ is capable of delivering a pinch which hurts for hours. We laughed, and continued,

"¿Usa este?"

"¡Si para pintura—rojo, azul, negro, amarillo!" "Yes, for paint, red, blue, black,
yellow!"

Since the horn worm is little besides skin covering a large amount of masticated datura
foliage, it is easy to see how it could be squeezed out like tooth paste to serve as a psychoactive
vehicle for various pigments. Perhaps the prehistoric slate palettes, which are too soft for
pigment grinding, but which still have pigment adhering to them, were used to prepare
psychoactive face and body paint for immediate application.

A local Tonto Polychrome jar on display at the Bullion Plaza Museum in Miami,
Arizona, pictures both the horn worm grasping a stem, and the Hawk Moth, which is its adult
form (Figure 8). In the evening during the monsoon months, the yellow flowers of the tall
Mountain Primrose, *Oenothera hookeri,* open explosively, feeding, first, the late-flying
hummingbirds, and then, as the evening darkens, feeding Hawk Moths. Next, the enormous
trumpets of the datura open, with their overwhelming fragrance. The Hawk Moths feed on the
datura nectar, and lay eggs on the datura which hatch into horn worms. Horn worms feed on the
datura leaves, and then, after chewing off the hard scute on their posterior, crawl to the ground
where they pupate in the soil, finally emerging as new Hawk Moths. The horn worms are so
voracious that they can strip a small plant, but mature daturas grow roots so enormous that they
can withstand being denuded. Primrose flower, primrose plant, datura pod, horn worm, and
Hawk Moth form an important icon unit for the sun's setting and moving into the underworld
(Figures 8, 18, 19, 20).

Sra. Mancinas was more interested in the caterpillar, than in the datura upon which it was
feeding. She was also much more interested in a picture of a Mountain Evening Primrose flower,
which she said was very good for circulation. Horn worms feed on Mountain Evening Primrose,
Devil's Claw, and Nightshade, as well as on Datura. All are medicinal plants, so the manner of
dosage in face and body paint is probably the same in each herb.

Datura

Datura wrightii, toloache in Mexico, is sacred to Xiutecutli, the Lord of Fire. Its leaves,
roots, flowers, and seeds are used for medicinal and ceremonial purposes. In small quantities it is
used to alleviate pain, as poultices on injuries, as an aphrodisiac, (Figures 17, 18) or to produce a
twilight sleep during difficult child birth. It can be used in divination to search out lost objects, or
to discern thieves. It can be used as an ingredient in flying ointment. In larger doses it can be
used to stupefy sacrificial victims so that they are manageable. It is used for vision quests, or for
initiations into adult status, where the participant is expected to forget childhood and emerge a
new person. It can produce shamanic trances, deathlike comas, or fatality. Datura is considered a
hallucinogen, but not a psychedelic. It is easily available, but dosage is hard to calculate. Local
doctors still treat overdoses among adventurous adolescents seeking a cheap high. The symptoms
of overdose include flushing, elevated temperature, the feeling of the skin being on fire, visual
impairment, irrational behavior, and terrible thirst. Apparently one problem with datura overdose

is that the victim may run off and throw themselves into a body of water and drown (Weil 1980: 171-172).

A safe dose is probably limited to face and body paint, topical application to relieve rheumatism, wound poultice, flying ointment, or smoking up to four leaves as an aphrodisiac. The "squash blossom" hairdress of marriageable young Western Pueblo women, and the "squash blossom" decorations of yarn-wound Devil's Claw, *Martynia,* pods on katsina masks, actually represent the datura flower (Rätsch 1998). Datura was, and is still, a commonly used additive to *pulque,* a fermented agave beverage, and to *tesgüino,* the Tarahumara maize beer (Rätsch 1998: 196-201). Devil's Claw seeds are still a folk remedy for arthritis.

Two well-preserved female burials, dating between A.D. 1475 and 1650, from the Zuni village of Hawikuh, excavated between 1917 and 1923 by Hodge, contained painted rods and datura branches. The Zuni workmen identified these as vertical side rods which supported a shrine covered with upright datura branches used by a medicine priestess in a curing ceremony for rattlesnake bite, Datura root, called *chi-kwi-mi-ne,* was also rubbed on the bite. The shrine included an upright stick, called *Ishina-kats-ikwa-ne,* with a painted wooden oval, representing the sun, from which issued a string with four pendant feathers (Smith, Woodbury, and Woodbury 1966: 214 – 218). This shrine may help explain the purpose of the paired painted wooden wands found in a less well-preserved state in Besh-Ba-Gowah and Pinal Pueblo burials. The earliest occurrence of these painted wand burials was 87b, a man over 60, who was the smallest found, standing only 153.47 cm (59.85 inches). This may indicate that the painted wand/datura shrine concept was brought by the early settlers from the north (see human stature discussion in Chapter 6). A rattlesnake icon appears on the left wristband of a high-status Mimbres woman (Figure 29).

The Zunis call datura *a-neg-la-kya,* after the little boy, who with his sister *A-neg-la-kya-tsi-ts* lived under the earth, but came out from time to time, and told the people above the earth how they could dream dreams and see visions. The Divine Ones thought this knowledge was disruptive, and banished them back into the earth, from which they now emerge as plants (Schultes, Hofmann, and Rätsch 2001: 106). Historically, only Rain Priests are allowed to collect and use the plant. They put powdered root in their eyes so they can see at night, communicate with birds, and petition the spirits of the dead to intercede for rain (Schultes 1972: 47). Today, datura is considered so dangerous that Zuni medicine men habituate themselves to its toxic compounds over time, and their followers drink their urine to obtain a safe dose (Richard Fisher, personal communication, November 2010), a practice which is still found in Siberia (Schultes, Hofmann, and Rätsch 2001: 83).

In northern India, the spherical, spine-covered fruit of the datura are strung into garlands as an offering to the Hindu god Shiva (Schultes, Hofmann, and Rätsch 2001). The same garland motif appears in Casas Grandes pottery (VanPool and VanPool 2007: Figures 4.1, 4.7, 5.1, 5.5, 6.3). Widely scattered Southwestern sites have yielded small globular jars with appliquéd spines which were apparently used to hold datura seeds or infusion (Huckell and VanPool 2006: Figure 9.4 and 9.5). At Gila Pueblo, small Gila and Tonto Polychrome jars with a spherical neck above a spherical body painted with datura pod motifs were used instead (Figure 18, center-right). A larger Tonto Polychrome jar with a bulbous neck and datura pod decoration, dating in the

Figure 17. Representations of Datura Use. <u>Top</u>: a figure with female genitals is pictured with a datura pod head within the outline of a large datura pod; Pinto Polychrome incurved bowl, ca. A.D. 1200-1300, Tonto Basin, Arizona, after Moulard 1981: Plate 95. <u>Bottom-left</u>: Mimbres B/w bowl design, male, with sunset and Milky Way motifs on phallus, standing on a caterpillar, after Davis 1995: 98. <u>Bottom-right</u>: Mimbres B/w bowl design, phallic Xhihutecutli-like figure with datura pod head and earrings, after Brody 1977: 190.

Figure 18. Datura Pod and Blossom Motifs. <u>Top-left</u>: Datura wrightii, seed pod. Scale: × 1. <u>Top-middle</u>: Mimbres B/w bowl design, after Davis 1995: 186. <u>Top-right</u>: Aztec datura glyph, after Rätsch 1998: 196. <u>Center-left</u>: datura motif painted on Tonto Polychrome jars from Gila Pueblo, A.D. 1440s, and on a Kechipawan Polychrome Jar, A.D. 1350-147, after Smith, Woodbury, and Woodbury 1996: Figure 49. <u>Center-right</u>: Sikyatki Polychrome bowl, A.D. 1375-1625, after photo supplied by Paul Kay. <u>Bottom</u>: Tonto Polychrome bowl from Kinishba, with red-centered datura pods flanked by white datura blossoms, after Cummings 1940: Plate VIII.

Figure 19. Hawk Moth and Monarch Butterfly Motifs. <u>Top</u>: eight Hawk Moths are shown with two trumpet-shaped datura blossoms, late Gila Polychrome bowl design, Kinishba, after Cummings 1940: Plate V. <u>Bottom-left</u>: Monarch Butterfly with sunflowers, Sikyatki Polychrome bowl design, after Hays-Gilpin 2006: 70. <u>Bottom-right</u>: Monarch Butterfly, Mimbres Polychrome, after Davis 1995: 193.

A.D. 1440s, was also found at Gila Pueblo. The identical datura motif appears contemporaneously on a Kepichiwan Polychrome jar dating between A.D. 1350 and 1475 excavated from Hawikuh (Smith, Woodbury, and Woodbury 1966: Figure 49, Plate 22).

Kinishba yielded well-preserved Salado polychromes (Figures 18 and 19), depicting Hawk Moths, datura blossoms, and datura pods (Cummings 1940: Plate V, Plate VII) and a Tlaloc goggle-eyed burial bundle motif (Young 1967: Figure 1).

Rea presents a detailed discussion of Piman attitudes toward datura, its shamanic and medicinal uses, and its connection with the traditions of the peyote quest and deer hunting (Rea 1997: 220-222).

Co-evolution Of Datura with Hawk Moths, and Milkweeds with Monarch Butterflies

Speakers of the Uto-Aztecan Language Group subscribe to a world view which deals with general classes of things which are narrowed down by amplifiers, both in the spoken word, and in art (Stone and Zender 2011: 10-28). For example, "flying things" includes birds, bats, butterflies, and moths. Pueblo Indians usually identify the flying insect motifs on prehistoric pottery as "Monarch Butterfly or Hawk Moth." Both are important in art, oral literature, and ceremony. Gary Nabhan (2004: 32) notes the co-evolution of datura and Hawk Moths and of milkweeds and Monarch Butterflies. Both pollinate and feed upon poisonous medicinals, which in turn protect them from predation, an arrangement known as mutualism. In Mexico, Monarch Butterflies are believed to embody the souls of the visiting departed (Alvarado 2012: 8-10). The Hawk Moths pictured in Figure 19, top, are associated with light-colored trumpet-shaped datura flowers, which are similar in shape to the datura flowers pictured with pods in Figure 18, bottom. The Monarch Butterflies are usually pictured with bright ochre-pigmented wings, and may be feeding upon sunflowers: Figure 19, lower. The spectacular flights of thousands of migrating Monarch Butterflies would put them in a special class even if their larvae did not feed on poisonous medicinals.

Figure 20. Mountain Evening Primrose Sun-going-down Motifs. <u>Top</u>: Mountain Evening Primrose plant growing from a ground line with pendant feather and rattle, male Mearns Quail decorated with Milky Way pattern and surmounted by horn worm, Mimbres B/w bowl design, after Brody 1977: 199. <u>Bottom-left</u>: blossom, scale ×1. <u>Bottom-right</u>: Mountain Evening Primrose buds in the process of opening, offset by Milky Way patterns, Mimbres B/w bowl design, after Davis 1995: 164.

Mountain Evening Primrose

The horn worm may feed upon the succulent foliage of the Mountain Evening Primrose, *Oenothers hookeri,* early in the summer. This tall, yellow-flowered plant is remarkable for the explosive opening of its flower on warm summer evenings. The four yellow petals begin to expand rapidly within the four sepals, forcing the bud into a diamond-shaped bundle held together only by the tips of the sepals. When the pressure becomes too great, the point of the bud is torn apart, and the fully opened flower appears instantly. Hovering hummingbirds and Hawk Moths swoop in immediately, to harvest the fresh nectar. This medicinal is still highly valued by the Tarahumara of the Sierra Madre Occidental for the treatment of circulatory disorders (Figure 20) (Sra. Conchita Mancinas, personal communication, March 2011).

Prickly Poppy, Wormwood, and Marigold

Tlaloc is associated with three sacred plants: *chicalote (Argemone mexicana),* Prickly Poppy; *iztauhiatl (Artemesia mexicana),* Mexican Wormwood, a medicinal used to promote menstruation, and to cause abortion (Rätsch 1998: 73-74); and *yauhtli (Tagetes lucida),* Marigold, a flower still used in Day of the Dead Ceremonies in Mexico (Oates 2011: 104). All parts of the prickly poppy are psychoactive: leaves, flowers, seed capsules, and dried latex. Prickly Poppy is associated with the underworld. The personator of Tlaloc painted his face black with latex and soot and spotted it with paste made from prickly poppy seeds (Figures 21, 22). Poppy seed was made into cakes in the shape of the Aztec sun god Huitzilopochtli which were broken up and consumed as a sacramental food. Medicinally it is used as a sedative, aphrodisiac, and euphoriant (Rätsch 1998: 61-63).

Tlaloc ruled over a verdant green heaven inhabited by those who had died from lightning, drowning, or "watery diseases." It was the opposite of the dry desert, and may be a version of the "flower world" which appears to be a major aspiration in Archaic through Salado cosmology. Western Pueblo friends tend to visualize their virtuous departed as being able to come back as rain clouds, and even place bolls of cotton on their faces in preparation for burial. They lay them away according to family custom, and then sit back and wait to see what happens. Hopefully, there will be some indication of their being accepted as cloud people.

A great deal of Western Pueblo perspective has seeped into local world view. During the summer of 2010 a neighboring rancher died. He had a liturgical service at a funeral home in Globe. As we left the service, everyone was delighted to see a rainbow, and commented happily on it. His remains were transported to the family plot in western New Mexico, where a graveside service was held. Midway through the service, it was interrupted by the congregation clapping and cheering. The officiant turned to see a cloud of butterflies and hummingbirds sipping nectar from the flowers on the casket. Everyone went home happy that their loved one had been accepted into a beautiful place.

Toad Poison

Although most psychoactive substances used prehistorically were derived from plants, a Mexican fresco depicts Tlaloc and Chalchihuitlicue presiding over a verdant paradise watered by canals supplied by a fountain gushing from the mouth of a gigantic toad (Oates 2011: 187). Toads occupy a place of honor in Mesoamerican art as early as 2000 B.C. (Figure 21). *Bufo marinus* is the giant toad of Mesoamerica. *Bufo alvarius,* the Colorado River Toad, is the giant toad of the Southwest (Oroc 2009: 108-111). It measures up to 7½ inches from nose to vent, and is very fleshy, about the size of a soup plate. Toads in general seem to produce poison from their parotid glands, partly to deter predators, and partly to make the water in which they breed unsuitable for the maturation of tadpoles of other species which would compete with their own young. Before the local mines broke through into an underground river and drained the canyons above Besh-Ba-Gowah and Gila Pueblo in 1929 (Carmen Malory Blalack, original agricultural patentee in Kellner Canyon, personal communication, 1954), the streams ran year round and were populated with fish, turtles, and various amphibians. Now, the only permanent water is in some of the deeper cow tanks. Nevertheless, Philip DeMario reports Colorado River Toads five miles by trail from Besh-Ba-Gowah in Russell Gulch in a reservoir and in a shallow well, which lie in the Salt River Drainage. I have seen a Colorado River Toad at San Carlos to the east, and my daughter, Stephani Poor, who lives south of Safford, Arizona, sees them often, when they burrow into her dog run to get into the dogs' water containers. Both these locations are in the Gila River Drainage.

Toad poison is very dangerous. My daughter, Stephani, once found her dog frothing at the mouth from having mauled a Colorado River Toad and rushed to remove it from the enclosure. The distressed dog licked her face and almost instantaneously Stephani lost her sense of balance and her vision blurred. She barely made her way into the house, and was down in bed for a day and a half. She and the dog survived. The toad hopped off the victor.

Toad poison can be milked from the parotid glands, dried, powdered, and smoked in very small quantities (Oroc 2009: 110-11). My daughter did not experience any pleasant or illuminating effects from her episode of toad poisoning. Drying and smoking may alter the effects of the alkaloids. For those who favor this hallucinogen, it appears to be similar in result to Magic Mushrooms, especially in its almost instantaneous effects.

Figure 21. Tlaloc and Giant Toad Motifs. <u>Top:</u> Tlaloc is standing in water with a winding water motif behind him. The poppy flower motif appears above his face which is blackened with latex, simplified from Rätsch 1998: 62. <u>Bottom:</u> Proto-Classic Maya giant toad with curls of poison emanating from its speckled parotid glands, after Miller and Taube 1993: 169.

Figure 22. Tlaloc as an Effigy. <u>Top:</u> a procession is led by a small figure carrying a goggle-eyed Tlaloc effigy decorated with water squiggles, Mimbres B/w bowl design, after Moulard 1981: Plate I. <u>Bottom-left:</u> Mimbres B/w bowl design, similar motif incorporated into a moth design, after Davis 1995: 192. <u>Bottom-right:</u> somewhat similar, Gila Polychrome bowl design from Kinishba, after Young, 1967: Figure 1.

Tobacco and Smoking

Nicotiana trigonophylla, Desert Tobacco, grows wild in the Southwest and northern Mexico. It is used by the Tarahumara as an analgesic, and by the Seri who believe that it has magical powers (Rätsch 1998: 391). The plants germinate after the spring equinoxial rains in late March, grow rapidly in April, flower in May, and have gone to seed and dried up by the end of June. Leaves on well-watered local plants are lanceolate, and up to 6 inches long and 2½ inches wide. Smoking tobacco may be prepared by slow drying, or by fermenting and drying.

Ritual smoking of strong tobacco can produce intoxication, but it is more likely that tobacco, like alcohol, was used as a vehicle for various blends of psychoactive substances. Tobacco smoke may be used to produce ceremonial clouds. Marigold, the "plant of the clouds" sacred to Tlaloc, may be infused for medicinal use, or smoked alone or with tobacco, and taken with peyote to promote visions (Rätsch 1998: 495-497). Tobacco was smoked in corn husk wrappers, in cane cigarettes, or in stone pipes. Alan Ferg recovered a stone pipe from his excavation of the south half of Room 111 at Gila Pueblo. This pipe has a long straight bore and is dissimilar to the coal carrier pictured in Figure 27, which has a cup in the top to hold the burning coal and a tiny hole extending up through the base to allow the passage of air. Smoking is depicted in Casas Grandes polychrome male effigies (Figure 23).

Peyote

Peyote found in dry rock shelters in Texas indicates its use there 7,000 years ago. Earlier use is indicated by specimens in a cave in Coahuila, Mexico, dating 8500 B.C. Spanish chroniclers report its use among many tribes at the time of the conquest (Schultes, Hofmann, and Rätsch 2001: 144-151; Pendell 2009: 86). True peyote, *Lophophora williamsii,* resembles nodules of unworked turquoise. It is said by several local people to exist on the lower, more desolate portions of the San Carlos Indian Reservation to the east of Globe. This is the "Peyote Button" of the historic Native American Church, where it is used as a sacrament, to heal afflictions beyond the reach of modern medicine, to gain visions, and for reconciliation.

Lophophora williamsii is the plant sought in the Huichol Peyote Pilgrimage. This pilgrimage is undertaken "to find one's life." Peyote is obtained by participation in an integrative guided meditation through a magical entrance into a difficult landscape which is perceived as beautiful, verdant, and blessed, and appears to be equivalent to Tlalocan, the heaven presided over by Tlaloc and Chalchihuitlicue. First-time pilgrims are blindfolded for a good part of the journey. This is in spite of the fact that it is no longer a 300-mile walk to peyote country in San Luis Potosi; it is a drive through traffic for much of the way. The approach is marked by confession of sexual transgressions and by tying a knot in a string for each. The string is burned, and the sins are forgiven. The first goal is a search for a land where water from small pools is dripped into gourds with a sacred arrow, an obvious fertility symbol. Barren women make the journey in the hope of having children, again a reference to the patronage of Chalchihuitlicue. The holy water is carefully carried home for use during the year. The music for the journey is made by drumming on the string of a hunting bow, and the hunt for the peyote is acted out as a

Figure 23. Pipe Smoking. <u>Top:</u> pipe recovered from Room 111, Gila Pueblo. It was made of black vesicular basalt/scoria, length = 4.5 cm, diameter of distal end = 3.0 cm, diameter of proximal/mouth end = 2.3 cm. It was drilled from both ends, meeting approximately in the middle; Arizona State Museum catalog # 82-45-181. <u>Bottom:</u> late Villa Ahumada Polychrome hooded effigy jar, Chihuahua, Mexico with pipe and *hikuli* motif on top of its head, after Moulard 1981: Plate 81.

deer hunt. After the cactus buttons are collected, and many eaten, they are carried home like deer from a hunt, and are blessed in the church. The participants experience spiritual insights, which are private and not shared (Furst 1972: 145-183).

Peyote, along with corn, is a gift from Mother Earth; deer, associated with the sun, is a gift from Father Sky. It is said that corn and deer nourish the body, and peyote nourishes the soul.

The counterclockwise spiral *hikuli* peyote icon found on Carretas and Huerigos Polychrome pottery from Paquimé, appears earliest in the Southwest as a Mimbres bowl design painted in the early A.D. 1100s (Figure 24). In the A.D. 1400s, it is rendered on the exterior of a Tonto Polychrome bowl from Canyon Creek Ruin (Crown 1994: 143). Between 1630 and 1670, it appears on the interior of a Hawikuh Polychrome bowl from Hawikuh (Smith, Woodbury, and Woodbury 1966: Figure 76). This last example incorporates the "X" roadrunner track motif which is used to symbolize the shamanic journey. The roadrunner is an important shamanic bird because, like the macaws and other parrots, it is hatched with one toe to the back and three to the front. Shortly after hatching, the outer toe migrates to the back, to form the "X" track, which looks the same in either direction. The whole point of the symbol, is that it is necessary to return from a shamanic journey by retracing ones path exactly the same way as one went, or one may not get back at all (Clara Lee Tanner, personal communication, ca. 1952).

The Huichol symbol for peyote is a rosette. However, Sra. Mancinas, the Tarahumara *curandera,* and Mrs. Joyce Montgomery, who formerly ran the Bylas, Arizona, trading post, both recognize the *hikuli* spiral as signifying peyote (Figure 24). The peyote Sra. Mancinas showed me was a white cylinder of dried cactus pulp, which appeared to be a peeled hedgehog or pincushion cactus, or perhaps Cawe or Wichowaka, which means "insanity" in Tarahumara. Cawe, *Pachycereus pectin-aboriginum* (Englm.), is a widely used medicinal which may be bought from vendors standing along the highway at cross roads in southern Sonora. In any case, there are numerous "false peyotes" which have varying potencies, and which resemble the *hikuli* design in that they have longitudinal ribs or rows of spines.

Peyote, real or false, is used to achieve individual spiritual insight, and in group worship. It is used by old and young without apparent ill effect. It is particularly useful as a panacea for body and mind, for increasing endurance for difficult tasks of communal labor, for long trips bearing heavy packs, and as a doping agent for foot races. Moderate use is emphasized, and in this context, it does not appear to be dangerous.   A sixteenth century statue of Xochipilli (Sho-chee-pe'e-ly), which was found on the slopes of Mt. Popocatepetl, depicts the deity as a shaman in ecstatic trance with his body covered with representations of psychoactive flowers. The platform on which he sits is bordered with cross-section designs of *Psilocybe* mushrooms. He is portrayed as the deity of inebriating flowers, including mushrooms. Miniature mushroom stones from Guatemala are 2,200 years old (Schultes, Hofmann, and Rätsch 2001: 62).

Figure 24. Hikuli Peyote Icons and Other Spiral Motifs. *Hikuli* motifs: <u>Top-left:</u> Huerigos Polychrome, after Fenner 1974b: 248; <u>top right:</u> Carretas Polychrome, after Fenner 1974a: 203. <u>Middle-left:</u> Hawikuh Polychrome, spiral with roadrunner tracks, after Smith, Woodbury, and Woodbury 1966: Figure 76. <u>Middle-right:</u> Mimbres B/w, after Davis 1995: 159. <u>Bottom-left:</u> Chalchihuitlicue pierced (impregnated) by a dart, holding her string apron in her left hand and a spiral centipede in her right, showing spiral womb icon and umbilical cord, after Pilles and Danson 1974: 21. <u>Bottom-right:</u> *hikuli,* reversed to fit outside of a Tonto Polychrome bowl, after Crown 1994: 143.

Magic Mushrooms

Both Fly Agaric, *Amanita muscaria,* and Teonanácatl (Divine Flesh), *Psilocybe,* grow on the Pinal Mountains above Besh-Ba-Gowah and Gila Pueblo. Local Yugoslavian and Italian mining families gather mushrooms on the first Sunday after the first full moon in August. The incompatibility of the sun and moon calendars make the date extremely variable, but, early or late, the trip still falls during the monsoon season when mushrooms are normally plentiful. The mushroom hunt is accomplished with a digging stick in the right hand, and a brown paper shopping bag with handles in the left. The mushrooms must be strictly fresh, since even a "good" mushroom which is beginning to produce spores will cause illness. As the mushroom hunters walk along under the Ponderosa Pines, the digging stick is thrust deep into the earth beneath a likely mushroom, overturning it. If it is fresh, and has no cup on the bottom, it is placed carefully in the shopping bag. Should there be a cup on the bottom, it is rejected as an *Amanita,* which is locally considered deadly, and not even touched.

The red, white-flecked *Amanita* is our reminder of when Santa was a shaman (van Renterghem 1995). *Amanitas are* still used by Siberian shamans for flying ointment. Siberian reindeer herders are greatly inconvenienced during mushroom season, when their mushroom
-eating herds dash about taking flying leaps, and scatter for miles in all directions (Vitebsky 2005: 138). Closer to home, Robert and I once went to the Kaibab Plateau to hunt deer during bow season. I spent an entire day lying in ambush, arrow on bow string, by a deer trail waiting for something to come along. Other than being bombed with Ponderosa Pine cones by angry squirrels, I saw nothing. Suddenly, a big Kaibab doe, taking flying leaps, almost flattened me. She dashed off, wide-eyed and be-mushroomed, never seeing me. Apparently, the Christmas song about grandma being run over by a reindeer is more truth than poetry.

Following the rule that all fresh mushrooms without cups on the stem bottom are edible, I have collected every color and description of mushrooms. One year, there were a lot of spindly little mushrooms which looked delicious, and I collected a good supply along with the more colorful types. When I got home I cleaned and sliced them, and began frying them in butter. I tasted little pieces as I worked. Suddenly, my perception shifted – everything was clearer! Brighter! And much more beautiful! My stomach was not upset, so the mushrooms went into the freezer, mixed with their less psychoactive cousins, and garnished our steaks all winter with no ill effect (Figure 25).

Mushrooms are delicious. Ravens eat mushrooms. Raven Shamans eat mushrooms (Müller-Ebelilng, Rätsch, and Shahi 2000: 173-175, 235, 240). It would be difficult for any deer hunter, or any gatherer of plant foods, to be unaware of the psychoactive properties of mushrooms. Considering that most deer taken by modern bow hunters are shot from ambush at a distance of only ten yards, it is hard to imagine that our ancestors, even during the Pleistocene, would have wasted time hunting deer or reindeer during mushroom season.

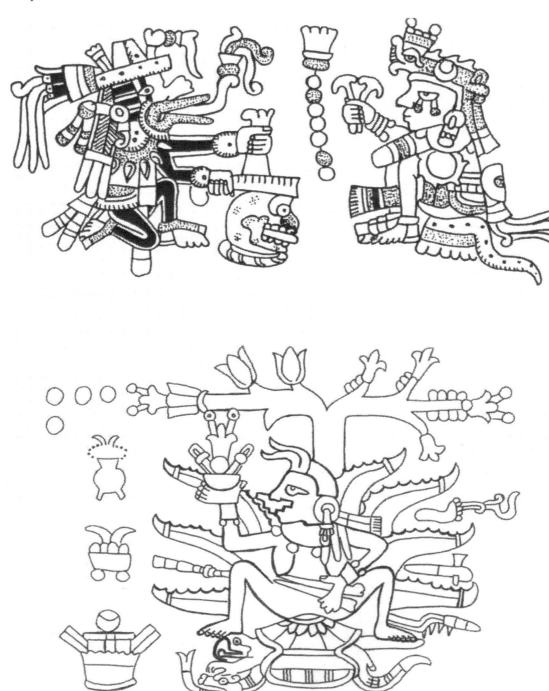

Figure 25. Magic Mushroom and Maguey Icons. <u>Top</u>: Ehecatl plays music on instrument made of human bone while God 7 Flower eats hallucinogenic mushrooms. Codex Vindobonensis, Late Postclassic Mixtec. After Miller and Taube 1993: 91. <u>Bottom</u>: Mayahual, Goddess of the Maguay. Codex Laud, simplified from Rätsch 1998: 44.

Maguey

Mayahuel, She of the Maguey Plant, is a goddess of the various agaves and of fertility (Figure 25). Pulque (Po'ol-kay), Agave beer, can be made from juice tapped from the heart of the living plant, from roasted agave hearts, from chopped fresh or boiled leaves, or from flowers. The *gusano de mescal*, a larva which lives in the Mescal Agave, is considered psychoactive, and may be legally obtained in Mexico in the form of lollipops. A dose of two or three worms, eaten whole, is considered adequate (Rätsch 1998: 44-47). Pulque contains only 3-4 percent alcohol, but may be fortified with datura, peyote, morning glory, *Psilocybe* mushrooms, or other plants. In addition to its use as an intoxicant, pulque is considered a panacea, and the *gusano de mescal* as an aphrodisiac. Agave juice has a sugar content of up to 8 percent, and a great deal of Vitamin C. Pulque is extremely refreshing, and was used as a payment for Indian labor by the Spanish

Colonials (Carlos Gaytán, personal communication, March 2011). Pulque was used during both shamanic and priestly ceremonies in Mexico. The fall of Paquimé occurred when the mescal roasting pits were full, suggesting the attackers took advantage of ritual pulque intoxication upon the occasion of the Spring Equinox, to overwhelm the pueblo. Similarly, the fall of Gila Pueblo took place during a celebration and market day when ritual corn beer intoxication on the occasion of the Fall Equinox would have placed the inhabitants at a disadvantage in defending themselves.

Wine can be made by fermenting the fruit of the Prickly Pear Cactus or berries. This can, in turn, be fortified with Magic Mushrooms or other psychoactive plants. Wine was and is brewed in southern Arizona as part of community-wide rain-making ceremonies. John Hohmann found brewing jars at the Ash Creek Site which still had an encrustation from the fermentation left on the interior; there was no doubt that alcoholic beverage was being produced, but the ingredients were not identified (personal communication, 1990).

Chocolate

Quetzalcoatl, in his function as patron of hereditary trading families, is associated with chocolate. It has been cultivated in Mesoamerica for four thousand years. The Aztecs considered cacao a food, a stimulant, currency, and a food for their gods. Chocolate was considered a tonic and aphrodisiac. Like tobacco, chocolate was mixed with a wide variety of flavorings and psychoactive substances (Rätsch 1998: 500-501). Today it is consumed locally sweetened and flavored with chili and cinnamon. In the prehistoric Southwest, consumption of chocolate appears to be documented from cylinder jars recovered from Pueblo Bonito, which resemble the tall, vase-like Mesoamerican chocolate frothing jars (Crown and Hurst 2009). Recent research suggests that holly, *Illex spp.,* products, used to make the caffeinated drink known historically in the Southeastern United States as "black drink," may also have been brought into the Southwest (Crown and others 2015). I am unaware of any evidence of chocolate in the area served by the Casas Grandes Trade Network.

6—Upland Salado Identity

Where Did the Upland Salados Come From?

When Emil Haury learned, in 1954, that my husband, Robert, and I were moving Robert's pottery business back to Globe, Arizona, he admonished me, "You really ought to do something about the Salado." In order to attempt to fulfill his expectations, I have spent many years trying to decide what Salado is. Salado is not pottery, though the Salados certainly made, used, and traded the Salado wares, particularly the Salado polychromes. This pottery series is based on the Mogollon brownware tradition. The clay paste is local brownware, the technique is predominantly coil and scrape, and the vessels are fired in an oxidizing atmosphere. In addition, the decoration tradition which became fashionable is polychrome, a northern invention. Therefore, I am led to suppose that the people who made the pottery are the women of a local Mogollon-like population, left behind after the Hohokam moved on to the San Carlos area, with a small addition of Kayenta settlers.

Salado and the Macaw Trade

Most archaeologists believe that Salado, whatever it may be, begins about A.D. 1250 and extends to about 1450. About A.D. 1200, after the high macaw usage at Chaco Canyon, followed by even higher macaw usage at Wupatki, there ensued a hiatus in the macaw trade. I have been challenged on my dating of the resumption of the macaw trade — at about A.D. 1275 — by some who feel it should be earlier, about 1250. Macaw bones available for study are securely dated as coming from sites which were settled about A.D. 1275. Better dating and future excavation will no doubt clarify the question. But, why should the resumption of the macaw trade coincide exactly with the beginning of the Salado cultural manifestation? Although there were plain brownware of the Mogollon tradition, Salado redware, and Salado polychrome macaw effigy vessels found in the Globe-Miami area, the only two macaw skeletons recovered were from a post-A.D.-1400 burial at Pinal Pueblo, and are assumed to have been kept for feather production, not sacrifice. The resumption of the macaw trade, in conjunction with the sudden heavy usage of buteonine hawks, appears to pertain to the beginnings of the Katsina Cult, rather than to the beginning of the Salado manifestation in this area.

Geographic Factors

The Globe-Miami Salados were "the people in between." They were positioned between the Hohokam of the Lower Sonoran Desert to the southwest, the Mogollon of the mountains to the east, and the pueblos of the Colorado Plateau to the north. More important than this diversity of neighbors seems to be the richness of their environment which provided them with wood, permanent water, arable canyon bottoms, and the opportunity to hunt and gather in the desert, the foothills, and the mountains without travel.

Post-Hohokam Pre-Salado Occupation

Between December 1987 and March 1989, Crary, Germick, and Golio (1994) conducted an archaeological survey of Upper Pinal Creek. Their data outlined a scattering of one- to two-room farmsteads, two- to ten-room hamlets, and few roomblocks during this period. Free-standing houses clustered around an unbounded courtyard were typical, as were piles of rocks indicating mescal roasting pits.

The Southwest is always dry. Sometimes it is drier. Faunal identification studies of collections from Archaic and farming sites suggest that if the population is small, and the rainfall is inadequate, humans will expand their hunting and gathering activities to survive. However, if the population is larger, inadequate rainfall cannot be compensated for by increased hunting and gathering, since the local wild resources are already incorporated into the economic system. I have come to suspect that, during dry years, the inhabitants of large local pueblos relied more heavily on the produce of fields irrigated by ditches leading from the year-round streams in the canyon bottoms than on hunting and gathering resources which would have been limited by drought. I discuss available resources in *Upland Salado Environmental Utilization* (McKusick 2013: 272-296).

No dry cave or rock shelter sites exist in the immediate vicinity of the Upland Salado Pueblos. Vorsila Bohrer sets forth the Archaic Period occupations of Fresnal Rock Shelter and High Rolls Cave, and neighboring dry sites in south central New Mexico, which have resources similar to those which were available to the Upland Salados. Bohrer's Table 2.3 (Climatic Record), Table 2.4 (Perishable Artifacts), and her discussion of "Dietary Elements from Fresnal Canyon Archaic in Pueblo Food Traditions" are particularly helpful in reconstructing models of local environmental utilization, the yearly round of activity, and cultural contacts (Bohrer 2007: 16, 19, 151).

An economic variable which is not often considered is altitude. The altitude of Besh-Ba-Gowah and Gila Pueblo is about 3500 feet. Four miles to the south, where I live, the altitude is 4000 feet. There are many plants that grow well at Gila Pueblo, which will not grow at all in my yard. Gila Pueblo receives sun all day; at my home in Kellner Canyon, there is no direct sun in the canyon bottom during the early morning and late afternoon. The closer one is to the Pinal Mountains, the worse and more frequent the hail storms, which are ruinous to squash. The most reliable and productive plantings in the area are small gardens cultivated in the arroyos just south of Gila Pueblo. They are sheltered from wind and hail, and serve as sun traps in the spring, allowing for early planting.

After more than 60 years of harvesting wild foods in the local area I have found that one cold, dry, La Niña year provides few berries and rabbits, and two La Niña years in a row is a real disaster. While wild plants and animals are plentiful throughout the area during warm, wet El Niño years, wild resources are not adequate to support a large population. In this area, at least, it appears that wild foods were extremely important, but that ditch irrigation is the factor which assured long term survival of the communities.

Stature

Probably the best indication of where the Salado came from is an examination of their bones. During the preparation of *The Gila Pueblo Salado* (McKusick and Young 1997), I computed stature reconstructions of all the local Salado skeletal material available for measurement using Trotter and Glesser's racial tables for estimating stature from length of limb bones (Anderson 1969: 127). It was sparse indeed, since local soil conditions deteriorate buried bone to the point that it crumbles when lifted from the earth. Reconstructed statures of seven men and seven women were calculated from Gila Pueblo, Pinal Pueblo, the Miami Sewer Project, and Besh-Ba-Gowah. The one sample from Besh-Ba-Gowah, a male, was of conspicuously different stature and build than the samples from the other sites. At 156.03 cm (61.43 inches) he was a stocky little man over three inches shorter than the other men and even shorter than the smallest woman in the combined sample. He was powerfully built in spite of his small stature, and similar in proportion to my modern Hopi friends. I included his measurement in the calculation, and still came up with a mean of 164.60 cm, or 64.80 inches. This discrepancy in size led me to wonder if the richly costumed people found slain on the roofs and in the rooms of the ceremonial/redistribution complex at Gila Pueblo were perhaps, because of higher status, better nourished and taller than the general population at Besh-Ba-Gowah.

In the spring of 2011, Alan Ferg, of the Arizona State Museum, sent me copies of Irene Vickrey's burial notes, room notes, and photographs. Fortunately, she had measured the long bones *in situ* before removing them. As a result, I was able to calculate reconstructed statures for 70 women and 28 men (as shown in Table 2). When the statures were ranked from shortest to tallest, there were null classes, actual gaps in stature, on the lower end of both males and females. Apparently, two populations were present, a few short, stocky people, and the majority of taller, more gracile people. Although the sample of short, broad, powerful people is poorly represented in Vickrey's measurements, they were conspicuously different from the tall, gracile people who comprised human skeletal material from the Globe-Miami Area, and comprised an easily discernable contribution to the early population of Besh-Ba-Gowah.

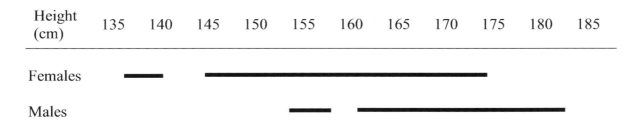

Table 2. Ranges for Besh-Ba-Gowah Stature Reconstructions

As can be seen from Table 3 comparisons, the people killed during the final attack on Gila Pueblo are similar in stature to the people from Pinal Pueblo and the Miami Burials. However, the Besh-Ba-Gowah statures, even with the very small people considered separately, form a demonstrably mixed population. The ranges are much broader, very low, and very high. The means do not match the medians and modes. The means for both Besh-Ba-Gowah males and females are conspicuously lower than the medians and modes, indicating that the population was not homogeneous.

Gavan's (1940: 10-12) comments on the skeletal remains from the original excavation at Besh-Ba-Gowah state that the population was short, not over five and a half feet in height. The reconstructed male mean stature for the general population of Besh-Ba-Gowah is 162.98 cm. The reconstructed stature of a high-status male burial excavated at Grasshopper Pueblo is 166.9 cm. The reconstructed male mean stature for Gila Pueblo, Pinal Pueblo, and the Miami Burials is 167.03 cm. The best matches for reconstructed Besh-Ba-Gowah mean male stature of 162.98 cm are Wind Mountain at 163.1 cm (Hinkes 1996: 385), Zuni at 163.5 cm, Laguna at 163.7 cm, and Hopi at 163.8 cm (Scott 1981: 133). Even though the Besh-Ba-Gowah population was mixed, stature was consistent with those recorded for contemporaneous populations.

Besh-Ba-Gowah Statures Below Null Classes

	Female (n=1)	Male (n=3)
Range	138.57	153.47-158.33
Mean		155.94

Besh-Ba-Gowah General Population Statures Minus Null Classes

	Female (n=69)	Male (n=25)
Range	145.17–174.07	160.00–180.05
Mean	162.77	162.98
Median	166.26	169+
Mode	160.65	169+

Gila Pueblo, Pinal Pueblo, and Miami Burial Statures

	Female (n=7)	Male (n=6)
Range	156.27–162.71	164.72–169.09
Mean	159.59	167.03
Median	160.27	167.04

Table 3. Stature of Globe-Miami Salados (in cm)

Facial Configuration and Build

Gavan (1940: 10-12) compared facial characteristics of skulls from Besh-Ba-Gowah, Kinishba, Tuzigoot, Swarts Ruin, Pecos, Puye, and Old Zuni. He found more similarity among the samples from Besh-Ba-Gowah, Pecos, and Old Zuni.

Zuni skeletal material is conspicuously scant. Therefore, there are three points of correspondence between the Upland Salado and Old Zuni skeletal material: stature, facial configuration, and slender build. Perhaps both groups are derived from the same early Mogollon stock. The presence of Salado Polychrome pottery at Hawikuh and datura iconography on a Kechipawan Polychrome jar, identical to that found on Tonto Polychrome jars from Gila Pueblo (Figure 18), suggests at least a trade relationship which continued to the fall of Gila Pueblo in the A.D. 1440s (Smith, Woodbury, and Woodbury 1966: Figure 49f; Plate 22h).

The burials from Besh-Ba-Gowah can be distributed in time by the absence or presence of painted pottery types deposited as grave goods. The shortest female, B-136, and the two tallest men, B-24e and B185b, were both from the early occupation of Besh-Ba-Gowah, between A.D. 1225 and 1325. Of the 20 shortest people at Besh-Ba-Gowah, only six were buried after A.D. 1325, and none after 1400. It appears that the population became somewhat more uniform as time went on, probably as a result of intermarriage.

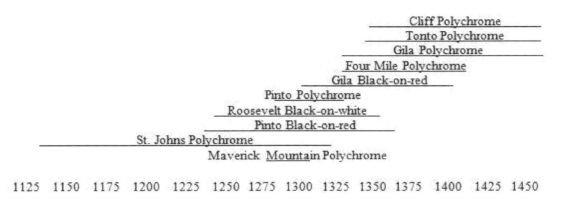

Table 4. Dating of Pottery from Besh-Ba-Gowah Burials.

There are no indications in the Besh-Ba-Gowah grave goods and stature data which lead me to believe that any ethnic group, ancestral group, or status group was better nourished than any other. However, trade ceramics included in burials suggest that the shorter stockier group may have been more likely to specialize in trading activities, both to the north and to the south, than the general population.

Indications of Northern Settlers Before A.D. 1260

Stature reconstructions of skeletal material, as well as several ceramic indicators, suggest that the population of Besh-Ba-Gowah was not homogeneous. The majority of the people from local burials were tall in stature, and slender and gracile in their youth. However, the Besh-Ba-Gowah burials included a few short, stocky individuals who were similar in stature and build to modern Hopis. This mixed population was not unusual in south-central Arizona at this time period. Surveys and testing by Archaeology Southwest indicate that very early, probably during the A.D. 1100s, settlers producing corrugated pottery moved from the Silver Creek area toward the San Manuel District of the San Pedro drainage (Clark, Hill, Lyons, and Lengyel 2012: 363-367).

Beginning in the late A.D. 1200s, after Besh-Ba-Gowah and Gila Pueblo were well established, people from the Kayenta Area, around Navajo National Monument, and from the Tusayan Area, around the Hopi Mesas and as far south as the Little Colorado River, began moving southwest to Perry Mesa and the lower Salt River Valley, south into Tonto Basin, and southeast, through Point of Pines into the Safford Basin and the lower San Pedro Valley. The Kayenta Area was left virtually depopulated, but the Hopi Area retained some population (Clark, Hill, Lyons, and Lengyel 2012: 374, Figure 6.16).

Ceramic evidence from New Mexico also suggests that the more general movements began earlier than the great drought of about A.D. 1275 to 1300, perhaps as early as 1225 or 1250 (Clark, Hill, Lyons, and Lengyel 2012: 374). The reasons for the earlier beginnings of these migrations may be warfare and political collapse rather than environmental change (Lekson and others 2002: 75, 92-96). This model fits well with the dating of Besh-Ba-Gowah, which indicates northern influence before A.D. 1260 (Figure 26)

Lyons (2004: 145) lists four traits as indicative of Kayenta migrants: the Kayenta entrybox, the perforated plate, the ritual disposal of raptors, and perhaps a kiva. Entryboxes, which involve a deflector and hearth in front of a floor level doorway, were not found locally. At both Besh-Ba-Gowah and Gila Pueblo, entry to the pueblos was across the roof. Rooms were entered through adobe-bermed hatches, by two-pole ladders centrally located over the fire pit. A unique feature of Gila Pueblo rooms is that the bottom step of the ladder was a raised rectangle of adobe, rather than a rung.

Raptor burial, especially of Red-tailed Hawks, is common in Salado sites. In addition to buteonine hawks, accipiters, eagles, and owls sometimes occur. A fragment of a Tonto Polychrome Barn Owl effigy pot was recovered from the excavation of Besh-Ba-Gowah (Figure 13).

Among the cultural contributions brought in by the Kayenta settlers was the perforated *puki* plate used in pottery manufacture (Figure 27). It is used as a base to hold and rotate a pot during its construction. Perforated plates are first known from a Basketmaker III site on Laguna Creek dating after A.D. 600. After A.D. 1250, they are found in major drainages of eastern and southern Arizona, from the Cliff Valley of New Mexico, and from Casas Grandes, Chihuahua. Their use continued during the popularity of Gila, Tonto, and Cliff Polychromes, that is until about A.D. 1450. Locally, perforated plates are present at Central Heights (AZ V:9:10 – ASM), Columbus Site (AZ V:9:57 – ASM), Hilltop Site (AZ V:9:68 – ASM), and Refugia Site (AZ V:9:59 – ASM), as well as Besh-Ba-Gowah (AZ V:9:11 – ASM), and Gila Pueblo (AZ V:9:52 – ASM) (Lyons and Lindsay 2006: 13, 15, 41).

Polychrome pottery has been demonstrated to be a northern idea. At Gila Pueblo a restorable Tonto Polychrome jar, dated at ca. A.D. 1440, was found with a broad, flat, upper surface, similar in shape and decoration to contemporaneous Salado Polychrome, and other polychrome vessels, recovered from the excavation of the Zuni village of Hawikuh.

Gila Pueblo yielded Maverick Mountain Series pottery, as well as Jeddito Black-on-orange pottery, from the Hopi Area. (Lyons and Lindsay 2006:22-27). Maverick Mountain

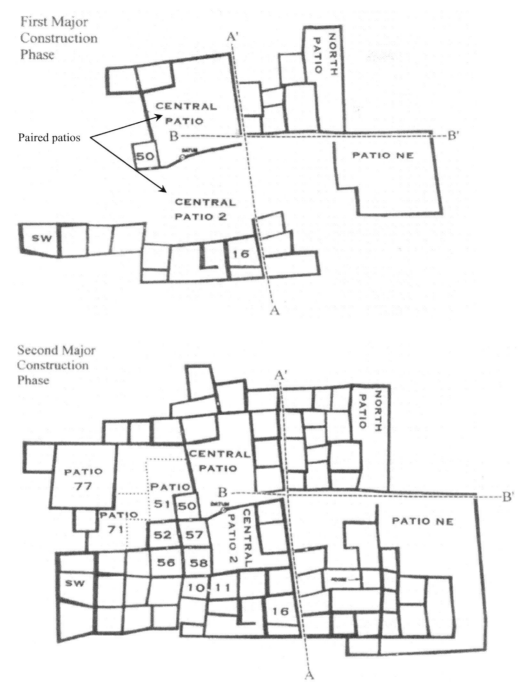

Figure 26. First Two Major Construction Phases at Besh-Ba-Gowah. Diagrams constructed from Alan Ferg's 1981 reconstruction from Vickrey's field notes (Arizona State Museum), and Hohmann and Adams (1992: 119-120). The three short persons who formed the below-null class were buried in SW, Patio 71, and North Patio by about A.D. 1325. Two quartering lines, A-A' and B-B' were established during the building of the earlier phase. The westerly end of line A-A' was terminated by the construction of the third phase, but B-B' endured throughout the occupation of the Pueblo. The most important construction of the second phase was a block of four interconnected rooms, 52, 56, 57, and 58, which were used until the end of the occupation, and which resemble the ceremonial/redistribution complex at Gila Pueblo.

Series pottery was made by northern settlers who arrived at Point of Pines about A.D. 1280. They were identified as being from the Kayenta area because they built a D-shaped kiva, grew distinctive types of corn and squash, and made northern-style pottery with local materials (Haury 1958: 1-6).

Another northern artifact recovered from Besh-Ba-Gowah is a small, centrally perforated, inverted cone-shaped coal carrier. When Hopi elder Oswald White Bear Fredericks visited the Besh-Ba-Gowah Museum in search of clues which might amplify Hopi understanding of their migration legends, he was delighted to see this exhibit. He recalled living as a small child in the home of his maternal grandmother, who was keeper of the hearth. Each night she banked the fire carefully, but in spite of her best efforts, it sometimes went out. Upon such occasions he was sent, coal carrier in hand, to the home of his paternal grandmother to bring home a living coal to restart the household fire. The coal was placed in the top, and the perforation through the lower portion allowed air to rise through it to keep the coal burning, and to keep the bottom from getting too hot to hold (Figure 27).

In my work in the Salado culture, it appears to me that northern settlers moved into southeastern Arizona at a period when scattered hamlets had already coalesced into larger settlements. Some of the newcomers lived in their own separate villages. Some joined local villages and lived in separate roomblocks. Others, like the local newcomers, seem to have lived within already existing roomblocks, but retained their identities, and kept ties, at least as trade relationships, with residents of the Hopi pueblos. Sometimes things went well, as they did here and at Grasshopper Pueblo. Sometimes they did not, and the Kayenta folk at Point of Pines were burned out after only about 20 years residence.

Indications of Northern Influence About A.D. 1275

E. Charles Adams (1991) has put forth a model in which the Pueblo Katsina Cult began among the Jornada Mogollon of the Middle Rio Grande and developed in the Upper Little Colorado and Salado Areas about A.D. 1275. It reached the Hopi area by A.D. 1350, where it was transformed and elaborated. He proposes that it served to integrate diverse populations present within agglomerated pueblos by redistributing food, supervising work parties, policing disruptive behavior, and facilitating exchange between pueblos. Briefly, it was a ceremonial construct which was expressed in icons, depicted in artwork and on ceramics, planned in rectangular kivas, performed in enclosed plazas, and advertised in ceramics and rock art. Knowledge of this religious complex may have come to the Upland Salado along with a small group of northern settlers, but appears more likely to be a later influence which accompanied continuing trade with the north. In any case, local depiction of a katsina mask on a very early Gila Polychrome bowl, dating ca. A.D. 1325 (Figure 27, bottom left) (Ferg 1982), suggests a trade relationship with members of the Upper Little Colorado development from ca. A.D. 1275 on, not with the later Hopi Katsina Cult, dated 1400-1450 (Adams 1991: 138-143, 157-158).

Since Besh-Ba-Gowah and Gila Pueblo were founded about A.D. 1225, and northern appearing building methods were used at Gila Pueblo shortly before 1260, it is likely that some northern settlers had already arrived and become integrated into the local economy before that time. This immigration appears to have occurred previous to the development of the Katsina

Cult. McGregor (1965: 423) reports a "rectangular kiva that had a platform at one end," which was found during the original excavation of Gila Pueblo. According to Hohmann, Germick, and Adams (1992: 101), "The room actually consisted of a large interior space with benches on three sides with what may have been an altar at the far end." From this description, it appears that the Gila Pueblo example is similar to the late configuration of the ceremonial room, Room 16, at Besh-Ba-Gowah. Room 16 is unique in that, instead of being plastered with brown adobe, the walls and benches were plastered with creamy white clay (Hohmann, Germick, and Adams 1992: 92-012). This is the same clay used to slip the interior of local Salado Polychrome pottery. It is available in a seam just down-canyon from Blue Tank, which lies between upper Ice House Canyon and Kellner Canyon. Mining and transporting enough clay to accomplish this task would have been an impressive endeavor. The distance is seven or eight miles by canyon-bottom roads, but there may have been a shorter trail across the base of the mountain.

Both Besh-Ba-Gowah and Gila Pueblo had compound walls and small enclosed patios which served as work and burial areas, but they lacked the large plazas associated with Katsina Cult performances involving long lines of dancers. Instead of a plaza, they had adjacent paired central patios. The patios at Besh-Ba-Gowah underwent several remodeling episodes, which accompanied six major building expansions (Hohmann and Adams, 1992: 109-124). It appears from Vickrey's lectures (Robert T. McKusick and John Woody, personal communication, ca. 1951), and from her field notes (Arizona State Museum), that these remodeling events took place following an earthquake in which "telephone pole-sized beams were broken and twisted like toothpicks," and "several raids" in which the pueblo was destroyed by burning. Gila Pueblo suffered a similar sequence of destructions and rebuilding episodes In fact, because of all the fires, Gila Pueblo is astonishingly well dated. The radiocarbon dating methods made possible by the burning, along with tree rings and archaeomagnetic methods provide us with secure dates for Gila Pueblo. It appears that the important commonality in all these rebuilding episodes is the presence of paired central patios, both at Besh-Ba-Gowah and at Gila Pueblo, which were suitable for work, trade, and other moiety-sized functions (Figures 26 and 28).

In addition to Besh-Ba-Gowah's well documented kiva-like ceremonial room, there was also an early-to-late complex of Rooms 52, 56, 57, 58, and connected ancillary rooms, which compare well with the ceremonial/redistribution complex at Gila Pueblo consisting of Rooms 101, 105, 110, 111, and connected ancillary rooms. Late in the occupation of Besh-Ba-Gowah, Room B/AB was used as a storage/vesting room for ceremonial costumes and accompanying paraphernalia, as indicated by the presence of an eagle claw, which may have decorated a costume, and a small food bowl containing bones of rabbit for moon, and quail for sun, along with roadrunner which has shamanic associations. There is no reason to believe that any of these rooms was connected to the Katsina Cult.

During the Eastern Arizona College excavation of the south end of Gila Pueblo, I was repeatedly asked if we had found any *comales*. A *comal* is a clay griddle which was used widely in prehistoric Mexico and at the Hohokam site of Los Muertos for cooking corn tortillas and other flat breads. We did not find any *comales*, but we did recover one fire-darkened *piki* stone. When Gila Pueblo Room 99 was built, ca. A.D. 1325, the hearth was rectangular, with three fire dogs arranged to hold a *piki* stone. At some time after the renovation of the pueblo ca. A.D. 1385, this stone was deliberately broken in half, and included with the grave goods for

Figure 27. Plain and Decorated Pottery Recovered from Besh-Ba-Gowah. <u>Top and middle</u>: fragments of a plain brownware perforated plate, reduced, and a plain brownware coal carrier (Scale: x1), both on display at Besh-Ba-Gowah Museum. <u>Bottom-left</u>: Katsina motif painted in an early Gila Polychrome bowl with an incurved rim recovered by Vickery, old adult female Burial 173, after Moulard 1981: Plate 96. <u>Bottom-right</u>: Ramos Polychrome effigy jar, from Chihuahua, Mexico, male Burial 110a, after Vickrey photo, Arizona State Museum.

Burial 9, a small infant, located beneath the floor of the north central area of Room 101, a restricted access area of the ceremonial-redistribution complex. The fire dogs were left in place in the original hearth, and a higher doughnut of adobe was built above them to accommodate a large, Cliff Polychrome cooking bowl.

A small shoe/boot "bird" pot was also recovered from Room 99. Dixon (1976), discussed in Adams (1991:79), suggests the form may have been used in cooking by thrusting the toe of the shoe between the fire dogs and under the *piki* stone. It may have been used to brew a beverage, or, more likely, cook a condiment which was served as an accompaniment to *piki*. The broad mouth is of a suitable size to dip a roll of *piki* into.

A larger vessel, the size and shape of a three-quarter-inflated football, filled with carbonized shelled corn, was found on the second-story floor of ceremonial Room 110. There was no cooking hearth in this room, so it probably should be considered to be a duck effigy. Both *piki* stones and boot pots are associated in time with Katsina Cult iconography on Fourmile Polychrome, placing their first appearance after A.D. 1250 (Adams 1991: 79-83).

While *comales* are southern, and *piki* stones are northern Arizonan in origin, the important thing is not the form of the cooking griddle, but rather a Mesoamerican process called nixtamalization, which makes corn more nutritious. To make hominy, dried maize is soaked, cooked in an alkaline solution, steeped in the cooking liquid, drained, and rinsed. The softened hull is then removed, and the resulting *nixtamal,* or hominy, may be used whole, ground to make tortillas, or dried and ground into flour for future use.

To make *piki,* blue corn is finely ground, and combined with boiling water to make gruel. To this is added strained juniper ash water, stirring constantly, and finally cold water is added to make a mixture like smooth pancake batter. The boiling water and the alkali solution swell and soften the starch grains and free the niacin, which prevents pellagra. The *piki* stone is heated, seasoned with crushed cottonseed, squash seed, or sunflower seed, and the batter spread quickly across the griddle surface. After a few moments, a paper-thin sheet is removed, folded, and rolled like newspaper. This delectable gray bread was a staple of pueblo diet, and is still made for ceremonial occasions in the Hopi pueblos (Niethammer 1974: 143-145).

Piki was and is an important component of feasting. Hayden (1990: 41, 60-61), suggests that through time, some persons, families, or other small units, became accumulators for the purpose of gaining status through gifting or feasting. This led to competitive feasting. In the local pueblos, the moiety responsible for the equinox observances, as opposed to the moiety responsible for the solstice observances, may be part of this pattern. Feasting foods are difficult to produce, and labor intensive, like *piki*. They are not produced as daily fare. Hayden suggests that such elements as consumption of tobacco, alcohol, fatty foods, and dogs are attributes of this conspicuous consumption. Brown (2013: 150-153) suggests that crops, such as squash, may have been domesticated because of their usefulness in feasting.

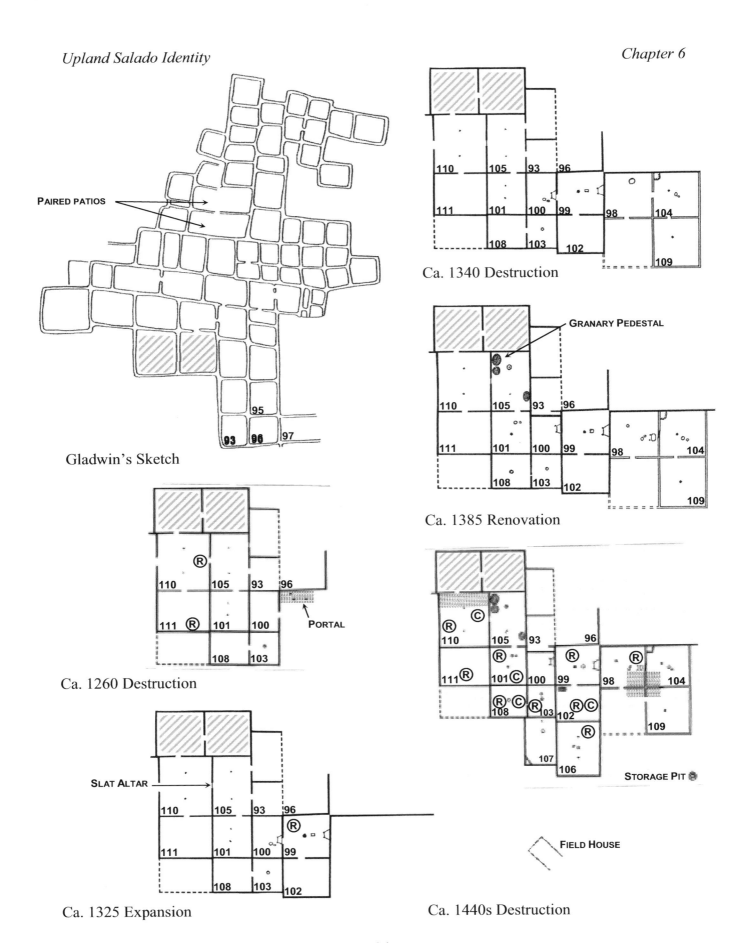

Gladwin's Sketch

Ca. 1340 Destruction

Ca. 1385 Renovation

Ca. 1260 Destruction

Ca. 1325 Expansion

Ca. 1440s Destruction

Figure 28. Successive Building Stages of the Gila Pueblo Ceremonial/Redistribution Complex. ® indicates portable religious artifacts. © indicates location of site-closing activities. To aid in visualizing how the complex changed over time, the same two rooms are shaded in each diagram. The room numbers included may also be of help.

       I would like to suggest that the exterior glyph pairs painted on Jeddito Yellow Ware bowls (Adams 2013: 113), and the decorative band painted on the recurved rims of Cliff Polychrome bowls, may have served to identify the person, or family, who provided that food for the feast, thus adding to their prestige. In any case, there was a free-standing corn storage room at Besh-Ba-Gowah, and quantities of corn, tepary beans, and cotton in the boll stored in the ceremonial/redistribution complex at Gila Pueblo. The Fall Equinox feast which was interrupted by the final attack on Gila Pueblo involved Cliff Polychrome bowls, and an enormous flaring Gila Polychrome bowl spattered with carbonized gruel like that used for the production of *piki*. There were also butchered and skinned dogs; single specimens of Common Bean, Sieva Bean, and winter squash; and a tubular stone pipe.

7—Upland Salado Social Structure

The Salado Life Path

The Salado life path is derived from information gained from Vickrey's Besh-Ba-Gowah burial records (Arizona State Museum), from the 1970s excavation of post-A.D.-1385 sub-floor child and infant burials, and from unburied family groups killed during the ca. A.D. 1440s destruction of Gila Pueblo (McKusick and Young 1997). My reconstruction of Salado life is also heavily based on illustrations of activities portrayed on Mimbres pottery and Pueblo ethnography related by Oswald White Bear Fredericks (Personal communication, 1973).

Birth

John Hohmann's group, which conducted the late 1980s excavation of Besh-Ba-Gowah, visualized Salado girls as having their first child at 13, and producing a child a year until they died in childbirth, or as the result of exhaustion, in their early 20s. But this is contrary to the conditions in farming communities in North America in the late 1800s, it is contrary to known reproductive patterns of non-literate farming and gathering people worldwide; and it is contrary to modern knowledge of reproductive biochemistry and process. First, we know from the muscle attachments on their bones, that both males and females typical of the area were slender and gracile throughout their youth and early adulthood. It was only in middle age, when they spread and took on more weight, that their joints and muscle attachments expanded to accommodate their increased size. The population, though healthy, did not take in excess calories. This lean physique leads to slow bone growth and slow maturation. Following Ellison's exhaustive work on fertility and reproduction (2001: 154-159), the girl must first grow up and then grow out. First comes stature, then comes the outward expansion of the pelvic girdle, and only then comes the maturation of the soft tissue, which in a society like the Upland Salado would occur at about 18 years. Even after menarche, the production of high quality ova, of viability adequate for the successful completion of a pregnancy, is not necessarily immediate (Ellison 2001: 221-226). Thus, a first birth could come as late as 19 or 20, which is in agreement with the estimated age of two pregnant women killed in the last raid on Gila Pueblo.

Miscarriage

A miscarried fetus, even a very small one, was usually buried beneath a room floor. The burial might have been elaborate, or there might have been no sign of offerings. This matter is considered further in Chapter 8, Religious Change.

Infancy, 0 to 2 Years of Age

The newborn was placed in a small cradleboard made of common reed stems, fastened to a rigid wooden framework. A premature infant buried at Gila Cliff Dwellings was placed on a fur-wrapped cordage blanket, and wrapped in scraps of what appeared to be out-worn cotton garments. In addition to plain weave, one piece of which had been mended or joined with a running stitch, were a fragment of brown on white tie-dye, and another with blue and brown embroidery (Anderson and others 1986: 218-221). The Canyon Creek infant (Haury 1934: Plate XLIV) is wrapped in coarse plain-weave cloth. Brown-on-white tie-dying is also found at

Canyon Creek (Haury 1934: 97, 99-10). When it became apparent that the infant was thriving, it probably went through a naming ceremony, and was given its own small food bowl. If it died, the food bowl was buried with it. Post-A.D.-1385 infant burials at Gila Pueblo were sometimes boot-shaped to accommodate the cradle board in the bottom, with offerings in the shaft. As the infant grew, it was given a similar, but larger cradleboard. At Gila Pueblo, infants were cared for by a six to seven-year-old child under the supervision of their mother or an old woman (Personal communication, Oswald White Bear Fredericks, 1973).

Early Childhood, 3 to 5 Years of Age

During this period the child played near where his or her mother was working with small pottery bowls and jars, pottery dog figurines, and real puppies.

Middle Childhood

By the time a little girl was 6 or 7 years old, she was tending a younger sibling, either a child in a cradle board or a toddler. At Gila Pueblo, she was within sight of her mother, or of an old woman. Presumably, a little boy of this age was accompanying his father to the fields, where he kept quail and rabbits from devouring the crops and perhaps even succeeded in killing a few small animals to be added to the family stew pot. He was also helping by carrying home fire wood.

If ceremonial practice paralleled modern Hopi usage, the child underwent his or her first initiation at 6 or 7 and received a new name. Some Hopi children undergo this initiation as early as 5, but this is a rare event involving precocious children who have evidenced unusual interest in spiritual matters, or who have had a spiritual experience. (Personal communication, Oswald White Bear Fredericks, 1973).

Later Childhood and Adolescence

The primary activities of womanhood in the Salado pueblos, basket and mat weaving, non-woven textile production, spinning, grinding, and *piki* making, were learned during this period. Gila Pueblo, at least, had an active soft goods industry. It is generally considered that it takes 12 spinners to supply one weaver. Spindle whorls made of perforated, rounded potsherd discs are found in both Gila Pueblo room fill and in women's burials from Besh-Ba-Gowah. The corn grown was a soft flour corn, not at all like the corn one gets at the feed store. Ability to grind fine corn flour and to make it into thin, rolled, flat-bread on a *comal* or stone griddle, were probably essential prerequisites for marriage. Each household had a metate inside its living room and another on the roof.

In addition to processing corn and cotton, a girl would also have learned to tend a kitchen garden of herbs and medicinals; to harvest cholla buds, prickly pear fruit, nuts, and wild berries with her mother; and to participate in large-scale agave harvesting and processing. An average living room had three mescal knives, hafted like a hatchet, but used like a saw to cut the sharp leaves from the mescal heart before it was uprooted and roasted in an earth oven.

This period was one of increased responsibility for boys, who were by now large and strong enough to take an active part in farming and hunting. Judging from Mimbres figurative pottery, they hunted with bow and arrow, and with rabbit sticks and nets; made snares for quail and other pests of the fields; and trapped fish in the streams. They would have also helped in the construction of rooms and in the operation of stone-filled mescal pits.

When they achieved adult stature and skills, but before the epiphyses of their tibias had completely closed at 18 to 22 years of age, both males and females appear to have undergone a second initiation into adult status. At Besh-Ba-Gowah and Pinal Pueblo, these fine specimens, in the flower of their youth, received the most elaborate burials of all, surpassing even those of venerable elders. Males of this group suffered more mortality as a result of stone arrow points remaining within their bodies at time of burial than the remainder of the population and probably should be considered warriors.

Men's household equipment included at least two stones axes per room. Only one plumb bob and one three-quarter-grooved adz were recovered. Two or three stone arrow points, and one or two arrow shaft straighteners, were found in each dwelling room. It is probable that most hunting of hares and rabbits was done with wooden field blunts which give a quicker and more reliable kill than a pointed shaft. However, stone tipped arrows were used for large game like deer, and for killing humans.

Adults

The average family appears to have consisted of a husband, a wife, children born at about three-year intervals, and an adult relative. Adults had the responsibility of upholding relationships with kinsmen, clansmen, society members, and trading partners. They kept the pueblo running as an economic unit, maintained its relationship with the powers that be, and also produced goods for trade to obtain desirable commodities not locally available.

Elder Women and Elder Men

The life of the elder woman begins with the end of the child-bearing years. Child-bearing begins late in societies where women do hard physical work and are also on low calorie diets. The highest fertility among women is between the mid-20s and the mid-30s. Low bodyweight occurring among women at any point during their reproductive years, whether as the result of hard work, of lactation, or of calorie restriction, may cause a cessation of menses. After the mid-30s there is also a decline in the function of the egg follicles and the number and quality of ova (Ellison 2002: 234-237).

In a society where there is no modern contraception, elder status in women is usually marked by a dwindling and cessation of menses. However, the apparent food use of cotton seed brings up the question of prehistoric contraception. Whether the inhabitants of Besh-Ba-Gowah and Gila Pueblo knew it or not, cottonseed contains a yellow dye which is an effective temporary male contraceptive, but which may also result in sterility. The inhabitants of Gila Pueblo may or may not have been aware of the mechanics of contraception, but a Pima myth that mentions a *kotdopĭ hiósig,* a datura blossom condom (Rea 1998: 131), indicates interest in contraception, at least in that group.

Males, unlike females, normally remain fertile late in life, so this may not be a diagnostic for male elder status. Whatever the norms at our sites were, old people were still valued members of society. They were a repository of information, wisdom, and ritual knowledge. A number of very old men and women, some of them with legs bent with age, were buried at Besh-Ba-Gowah. A very old woman, with a healed hip fracture, was found slain under a ramada on the roof of the second story of the ceremonial complex at Gila Pueblo, where she may have been spinning while she oversaw a nearby seven-year-old caring for an infant. Old women could still deliver babies, and could still take part in sacred women's matters. Old men could still weave, could still pray and sing, and could still tell instructional stories.

Kinsmen, Clansmen, and Trading Partners

Kinsmen are actual relatives, or adopted relatives. Clansmen are descended from the same legendary ancestor, have the same oral histories and traditional songs, and serve as hosts to visiting clansmen from another pueblo. Trading partners are engaged in a long-term commercial relationship and, while they may not be invited to stay in one's house, they may camp next to it.

White Bear checked in several times on the 1970s Gila Pueblo excavation, and subsequently on the displays there and at Besh-Ba-Gowah. According to White Bear, Hopi migration legends mentioned that half of the population of Tonto Cliff Dwellings moved to Hopi, but there was no mention at all that people from the Globe-Miami area had done so. Conversely, it seemed to him that people from the Hopi Area were present in our Upland Salado sites. -This opinion agrees with the evidence for a Kayenta group at Besh-Ba-Gowah (compare to Tables 2 and 3).

Hereditary Status and Moiety Membership

Information about Upland Salado social organization is derived from hundreds of pages of Irene Vickery's room reports and meticulous burial records, from reports presented at the Second Salado Conference (Hohmann, Germick, and Adams 1992: 92-102, Hohmann and Adams 1992: 109-124), Hohmann's statistical analysis of Besh-Ba-Gowah burials (1992a: 424-494, 505-518, 529-558, 570, 580-649), McKusick (1992: 86-91), and from *The Gila Pueblo Salado* (McKusick and Young 1997). The principal of complementary duality which is evident in the dual functionaries, the midwife and the shaman, first appears in the Old World Upper Paleolithic (compare Old World Beginnings in Figures 1 and 2). In the New World, dual division in village layout is found in northern Mexico about 1500 B.C. Dual division of pueblos contemporaneous with Besh-Ba-Gowah and Gila Pueblo is evident at Grasshopper Pueblo (Reid and Whittlesey 1999) and Kinishba, both of which are split by major arroyos. The modern pueblo of Zuni also has a dual layout and function. Prehistoric villages of southeastern Arizona are divided by ceremonial racetracks (Di Peso field trip, 1952). Rea (2007a: 15-16) presents a helpful summary of the place of moieties in Piman cosmology.

Since modern pueblo peoples operate on a matrilineal, matrilocal basis, it is reasonable to speculate that their forbearers also did so. This system is based on descent through a female lineage which owns the property, including house and fields. The eldest female is generally the head of the extended family, assisted by her eldest brother. Women, and their children, tend to remain in the general matrilineal room suite; whereas men tend to marry into the household of their wives, while still retaining a strong relationship with their birth family. My model of high-status leadership at Gila Pueblo is based upon ethnographic comparison to the social organization of historic Western Pueblos. The richly clothed persons at Gila Pueblo were possibly members of a female lineage in which the older man, usually a brother of the ranking female, instructs a younger successor, usually his nephew. In addition to these hereditary relationships, both men and women can also join one or more sodalities, or voluntary organizations, which serve to knit together the various lineages which made up the village.

For convenience in considering hereditary organization and status, I have divided the pueblos into moieties, designating the people living in the east half of Besh-Ba-Gowah and the south half of Gila Pueblo as "Summer People," and those living in the west half of Besh-Ba-Gowah and the north half of Gila Pueblo as "Winter People." These designations took form in my mind as the result of my faunal identifications from the roomblocks on each side of the Salt River draw at Grasshopper Pueblo (McKusick 1982: 87-96). I proposed a model in which the inhabitants of the eastern roomblock were descendants of pueblo peoples who came in as settlers from the Colorado Plateau, brought with them Large Indian Domestic Turkeys, built a large reservoir upstream from the pueblo, and appeared to be most interested in farming. I have always thought of them as "Summer People." The families living in the larger roomblock, west of the draw, seemed to have been indigenous people of Mogollon ancestry who hunted wild turkeys instead of raising domestics, and were, to judge by their garbage, most interested in hunting and gathering. I have always thought of them as "Winter People."

Obviously, it was necessary for everyone in pueblo society to be gainfully employed all the time, but even so it is possible to vary supervision by season. My model suggests that the leadership of the "Summer People" at Gila Pueblo governed group farming activities from the Spring Equinox to the Fall Equinox, concluding with a general ceremonial celebration on or about September 21. Their responsibilities would have included maintaining reservoirs for domestic water use, cleaning irrigation ditches, calculating the proper times to plant, cultivate, harvest, and store crops, the songs and observances necessary to ensure their growth, and the manufacture of items resulting from their efforts, such as cotton cloth and corn beer for the fall festival. Probably the most important decision to be made each year was how much acreage to devote to corn production, versus how much acreage was to be planted in cotton to produce fiber for the soft goods trade. This issue could be decided by determining the depth of snow pack on the Pinal Mountains which dominate the southern skyline.

As with the inhabitants of Grasshopper Pueblo, I visualize the leadership of the "Winter People" at Gila Pueblo as having been responsible for the supervision of group activities from the Fall Equinox to the Spring Equinox, culminating in a spring festival about March 21. Their areas of responsibility would have included supervision of hunting, processing, and preserving the meat of big game animals, the songs and ceremonies necessary to ensure successful hunts, the planning of group hunts for the production of rabbit skin-cordage robes, and seasonal large scale harvests of agave hearts which were roasted, sliced, dried, and also brewed to produce *pulque* for the spring festival.

Hohmann's group, which re-excavated and stabilized Besh-Ba-Gowah, presented a model (personal communication, 1990) in which their "Winter People" were responsible for the Winter Solstice ceremonies, and their "Summer People" were responsible for the Summer Solstice ceremonies. We all agreed that the architecture of the two sites suggested that they operated in complementary duality, alternating in the presentation of the four main solar festivals of each year for the benefit of both pueblos and the surrounding smaller settlements.

Ceremonial Costumes of Summer Moiety Leaders

The people slain on the roofs and in the rooms of Gila Pueblo at the Fall Equinox celebration in ca. A.D. 1440 were in great contrast to each other. Of the 70 persons slain in the rooms excavated by myself and Eastern Arizona College students, 63 were completely unadorned, one wore brush chaps, and six were elaborately costumed. The six comprised two groups, each consisting of an older man, a younger man, and a woman, and may represent my two proposed moieties.

The males from the group which appears to hold hereditary status (a male elder, and a nephew in training as is common in pueblo society), and to represent the "Summer People" Moiety, wore cloth medicine pouches suspended from their belts on their right hips. The elder died, shot in the back with two arrows tipped with triangular points, one of obsidian, and one of chert, like those produced at the Armer Ranch Site. He fell in the southeast corner of Ceremonial Room 110, where he lay with his chest supported by a large storage jar, and his legs and forearms resting upon the floor. He was holding a carbonized shaft at least 40 cm. long, which appeared to be the remains of a lance, in his right hand. This lance was tipped with a beautifully flaked, wood-grain, Tiger Chert biface (Figure 29, left) (compare Crotty 2001: Figure 4.10).
Other wood-grained bifaces of exceptionally fine manufacture have been recovered from sites yielding Salado polychromes such as Cutter Ruin (AZ V:10:4 - ASM), Point of Pines (AZ W:10:50 - ASM), and the Safford area to the east; Q Ranch Pueblo (AZ P:13:13 - ASM) to the north; Gipe Site (AZ N:16:6 - ASM) to the northwest; and Kinishba (AZ V:14:1 - ASM) to the northeast. Another specimen came from the Henderson Site (LA1549 - MNM), near Roswell, New Mexico. Raw material sources for the production of these bifaces appear to be northwestern Colorado or southwestern Wyoming. They may have been traded in already-formed as elite and/or ceremonial goods. Large bifaces are uncommon in southeastern Arizona sites, but were and are highly valued by historic pueblo groups, particularly as ceremonial paraphernalia (Ferg 1988:214-218; Whittaker, Ferg, and Speth 1988).

The carbonized plain-weave cotton medicine pouch worn by this older man contained six carbonized kernels of corn, a spherical red quartzite concretion, a quartz crystal, and a flake scraper made of gray-banded chert. A Tonto Polychrome male human effigy jar (Figure 29, upper-right), which appears to depict an elder personage, was recovered from Room 103. The jar originally had feet that had been broken off long before the fall of Gila Pueblo, and each side of the top of the jar was drilled for suspension. The ears were pierced, but no ear pendants were

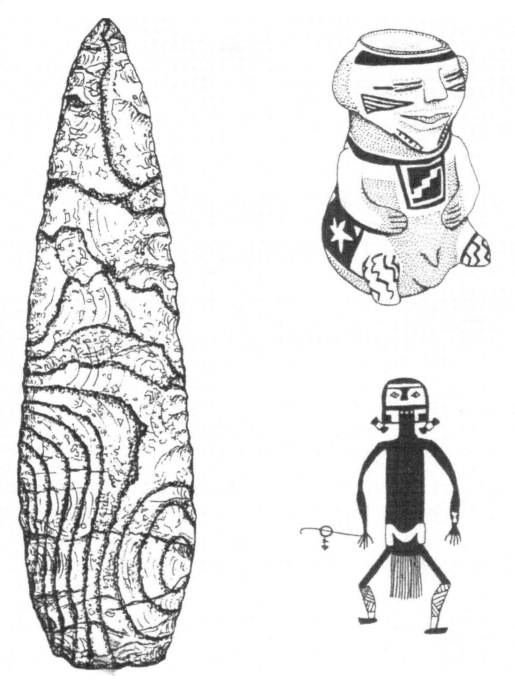

Figure 29. Costumes of Gila Pueblo Summer Moiety Leaders ca. A.D. 1440. Left: stone biface found with the elder male slain in Room 110, Scale: ×1. Top-right: Tonto Polychrome human effigy jar found in Room 103 portraying a personage with a medicine pouch on his right hip. Another is suspended from his neck.. Bottom-right: Mimbres woman wearing a shell bead stomacher over a string apron (after Bradfield 1931: Plate 79, No. 364), which duplicates that of the high-status woman found in Room 110. A rattlesnake icon appears on her left wrist (see Figure 7). She may be a rattlesnake curandera.

found. The personage depicted wore a loincloth and blanket decorated with a cloud step pattern, footless stockings, a beard, face paint, and a medicine pouch on his right hip, ornamented with a multipointed star in negative. This motif is associated with CeÁcatl, the Morning Star Warrior (Figure 3) (Day 1992: 56; Burland and Forman 1975: 36-37).

The younger man of this group lay face down on the roof above the wall separating Room 99 and Room 102. Beneath his chest was a spherical stone ball, 6 cm in diameter. Zuni, Hopi, San Ildefonso Pueblo peoples, and Apaches enclose stone spheres of this type in rawhide to attach them to clubs in a free-swing manner (Gifford 1940: 33). The shaft is commonly about 40 cm long, and is pierced on the lower end for a strap which passes around the wrist of the user. Alan Ferg found two more stone balls during his excavation of the south half of Room 111. One, 6.5 cm in diameter, was an unmodified quartzite cobble. The other, 8.3 cm in diameter, is a minimally altered hematite sphere (Ferg, personal communication, 1988). Both were suitable for use as rawhide-covered club heads.

The medicine pouch worn by this youth held a chalcedony "desert rose," an obsidian nodule, a quartz crystal, a copper bell, and a Clovis point which is similar in size and shape to the one recovered from Ventana Cave (Haury 1975 : v, 179-180).

The third person who appears to belong to the "Summer People" Moiety leadership group is a mature woman wearing a crimson string apron adorned with a stomacher of 6000 to 7000 fine *Laevicardium* shell beads caught up at each side by what appeared to be middle ear bones of a toothed whale (compare Figure 29, lower-right). The middle ear bones of toothed whales are only attached to the skull by tendons and connective tissue. They are very dense, and wash up on the seashore like pebbles. Some of them have natural holes through them, making them useful as beads or pendants (Koerper, Hunter, Snyder and Cramer: 2014; Koerper and Lipps: 2015).

Her string apron, protected from the fire by a thick layer of beads, was much too brightly colored for vegetable or mineral colorants. The color was a good match for cochineal. Cochineal insects still feed on the Prickly Pear Cactus in the area; and when a hard winter freeze kills them, brilliant red streaks stream down the cactus pads from their bodies during the early spring rains.

This woman was probably killed on the roof, carried to Room 110, and formally laid out on her back before the slat altar, feet to the east and head to the west, as though she were an altar piece. Even with her right shoulder lay an infant in a reed cradle board. Even with her left shoulder lay a six- to seven-year-old child. This woman and her two children were probably from an important lineage to have been recognized among the dead, and formally laid out as part of a site-closing ceremony by whatever survivors or neighbors arrived to formally close and burn the decimated pueblo.

Ceremonial Costumes of Winter Moiety Leaders

The leadership of each moiety appears to have consisted of a large elder male, a younger male, and a mature woman. Artifacts found with three such persons are illustrated in Figure 30. The body of the elder man associated with the "Winter" Moiety lay on the ground-level floor of Room 105, the most inaccessible room in the section of Gila Pueblo excavated in the 1970s. He lay on his right side, shot in the back with an arrow tipped with a triangular white chert point (Figure 30) penetrating his chest cavity, his head smashed with a large metate. He had apparently been looking up when the final blow came, as his neck broke and his face was oriented toward his back. A small double-bitted axe, which in local Salado sites is considered a weapon rather

than a tool, lay at his right shoulder (compare Le Blanc 1999: 108, Figure 3.6; 113). Axes may be used as both tools and weapons, but small double-bitted axes such as the one illustrated in Figure 30, are rare; found in special usage proveniences; and are unlike the large, single-bitted utilitarian axes found in profusion in the sites. Both small double-bitted axes, the ball-shaped club head, and the Tiger Chert blade recovered from the Ceremonial-Redistribution Complex at Gila Pueblo, were located in a position consistent with being held in the right hand. Two bone hairpins were in place at the top rear of the elder male's head, probably inserted in a large knot of his hair. The smaller, made of the shaft of a deer metapodial, is elliptical in cross-section, sharply pointed, with a squared-off head. The larger pin was made from the shaft and proximal head of a Whitetail deer tibia. Both had a hole drilled in the top end, probably to anchor a feather and/or fiber ornament, such as are illustrated on a man in a bat costume in a Mimbres bowl (Figure 13, lower-left, and Figure 30, upper-right). The pins were not only similar in form, but also were worn in the same position and placement. A similar, but far more elaborate, drilled hair pin was recovered from a Santa Cruz Phase cremation at Snaketown (Haury 1976: 303, Figure 15.4). Bone awls/hair pins with holes drilled into the proximal end of the bone are commonly found in Sinagua sites, as well (McGregor 1941:227).

One of the many people killed on the roof was a large younger male who lay on the southwest corner of the roof of Room 100 and the adjoining roof of Room 101. This man wore a large hairpin similar to the one in Room 105. In addition he wore jewelry of dog whelks. . The string holding the shells had burned through, and they rolled down the slope of the collapsed roof, but they were most probably from a bracelet on his left wrist. A similar artifact is pictured by Fulton and Tuthill (1940: 38).

An interesting feature of the hairpins is that they were completely permeated with hair oil. Permeation with hair oil gives bone artifacts a translucent appearance when they remain unburned and the appearance of ebony when burned. This permeation suggests they were probably worn all the time, year after year, such as those I identified, which were found with a tall, high-status male buried at Grasshopper Pueblo compare Griffen 1967: Figure 7).

Second-story Room 101 was entered from the roof by a hatch, and provided the only access to ground-story Room 101 beneath it, which in turn provided access to Room 105, where the elder of this group was killed along with nine other persons who had fled there. Beneath the floor of Room 105 was the highest status infant burial in the complex.

An older, heavier bodied, female of this group was found on the second-story floor of Room 111, beneath the hatch. She wore a heavy necklace made of graduated shell beads like those depicted in Mimbres pottery design (Figure 30, lower-right).

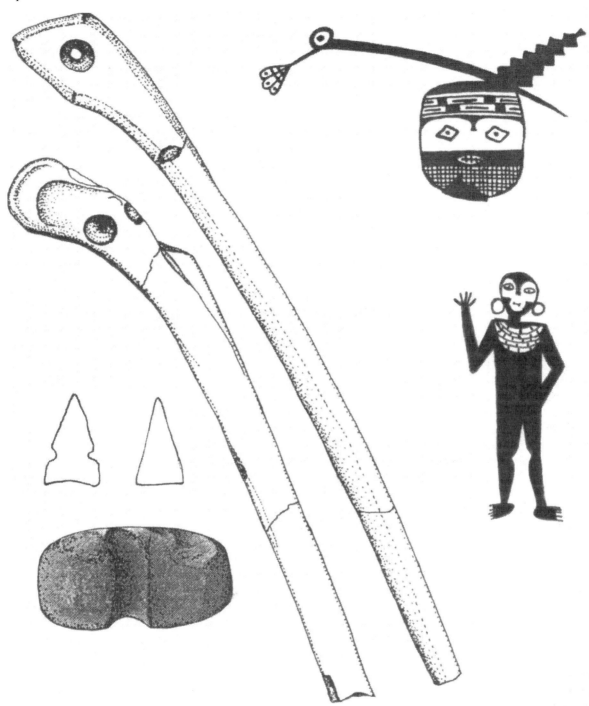

Figure 30. Costumes of Gila Pueblo Winter Moiety Leaders ca. A.D. 1440. Top-left, extending to the middle bottom: views of hairpins made from White-Tailed Deer tibiae: left-most: from the roof of Room 101; Center: from Room 105; Scale ×1. Top-right: Mimbres depiction of same type of hairpin (Brody and others 1983: Figure 6) with what may be the tail of a hummingbird tied to it (McKusick 2001: Figure 44). Middle-left: notched local Salado point and triangular Amer Ranch type point, Gila Pueblo, Scale x 1. Bottom-left: double-bitted axe, apparently an insignia of rank (Barnett 1973: 27-I, 28); Hagen Site, Scale: x 0.45. Bottom-right: Mimbres B/w depiction of woman wearing graduated shell bead necklace like that from Room 111, after Brody 1977: 50.

Sodalities

In addition to hereditary relationships, which include both male and female members, a Pueblo person can belong to one or more sodalities. Burial information from Grasshopper Pueblo indicates that a person may belong to none, to one, or to more than one of these organizations (Reid and Whittlesey 1999: 126-132). These voluntary organizations may involve only one gender, or may have complimentary dual single-gender halves, like our contemporary Masonic and Eastern Star organizations. Sodalities which appear to be present at the Upland Salado Pueblos are a Hunting Society and a Warrior Society for the men, and a Woman's Society which may have worked in complementary duality with the Warrior Society.

If we accept that the people who reoccupied Gila Pueblo in 1345 originated in the local, small, hilltop pueblos which were vacated at that time, it is probable that there was an excess of persons accustomed to community leadership. Since the community was coalescing at that time it may be the persons more schooled in ceremonial knowledge undertook leadership of the moiety structure of the reorganized pueblo, and the others found purpose in sodality leadership.

Costume of the Hunting Society Leader

Another relatively high-status was represented in both the destructions of ca.1340 and the 1440s by the presence at each event, of a single, large, tall man associated with the ceremonial/redistribution complex. Both men, a hundred years apart in time, wore what may have been brush chaps fastened along the outside of the leg by single conus shell tinklers, used as toggles, at the hip, thigh, knee, calf, and ankle. Leg coverings such as these are worn by hunters depicted on Mimbres B/w and Tabirá Polychrome pottery (Brody, 1977: Figure 115; Hayes and others 1981: Figure 114e).About A.D. 1340, the roofs and walls of Gila Pueblo were brought down in moments as the result of a severe earthquake, which made the pueblo vulnerable to attack by enemies who seem to have been waiting for just such an opportunity. Some inhabitants were crushed by debris from the earthquake, but two men were trapped by the wreckage where they had taken shelter in doorways. One of these was a tall man caught in the west doorway of Room 110. Rescuers who were apparently attempting to free him were struck down in the post-quake attack and the pueblo was set ablaze. The arrow points used in this massacre were of local manufacture. The conflict may have been an opportunistic response to the residents of Gila Pueblo drawing off too much irrigation water for its broad fields, causing a shortage for Besh-Ba-Gowah and Pinal Pueblo which lay downstream. The man who was incinerated in the doorway had *Conus* shell tinklers around his lower legs, which appeared from their positions to have been toggle fasteners for brush chaps.

At the A.D. 1440s destruction of Gila Pueblo, the tallest mature man, who had a healed tibial injury, lay on the roof of Room 105. He also had *Conus* shell tinklers (such as the one illustrated in Figure 32), positioned at the hip, the thigh, the knee, the calf, and the ankle. Again these appear to be toggles to fasten brush chaps, which in this environment, where there are many species of thorny shrubs, would be a necessity. The large size of these men, and their association with the ceremonial/redistribution complex, suggests that they may be leaders of a hunting sodality. These utilitarian usages of single, widely spaced, *Conus* shell tinklers, apparently employed as toggles, are different from clusters of tinklers attached to wands or clothing, suspended from the neck, or attached to the waist, arm, or leg. Clustered tinklers produce a clatter as the wearer moves (DiPeso and Fenner 1974: pp. 467-468). Clusters of tinklers were recovered from Besh-Ba-Gowah burials.

Men wearing shell-fastened chaps in ca. A.D. 1340, and later, in the 1440s, and the costumes of the suggested 1440s moiety leaders, which are like those painted on Mimbres bowls in the early A.D. 1100s, demonstrates a remarkable conservatism in outward symbols of socio/politico/religious structure.

The heavy equipment operator, who leveled the Hagen Site for subdivision construction, inadvertently destroyed what appeared to be a hunter's shrine containing deer and other bones penetrated with projectile points of local manufacture (Figure 35).

Warfare and Warrior's Society

Warfare, in the form of presumed slave raiding by people using Armer Ranch projectile points occurred at Gila Pueblo ca. 1260 and in the 1440s. An attack with the intent of annihilation by people using locally made Salado projectile points occurred at Gila Pueblo ca. 1340 immediately following an earthquake. Vickrey noted "several" attacks with burning at Besh-Ba-Gowah, but did not suggest their cause, other than that an earthquake was involved in one destructive incident.

In the early days of the occupation of Gila Pueblo, work was done under ground-level ramadas and under a portal built against the south wall of Room 96, which adjoined a ground-floor doorway into Room 100. After the destruction of 1260, ramadas were moved to the pueblo roof, which was provided with a knee-high balustrade along its outer edge. The ground floor door was also sealed.

It is important to note that in 1260, the south wall of Shiner's Room 96 was an informally built adobe compound wall, which was incorporated into the roomblock as room building expanded. Therefore, Gila Pueblo had a compound wall before 1260. In the 1440s, the compound wall was south of the structure, leaving space between the wall and the very late jacal rooms. It's position may still be observed north of the edge of the south parking lot. Compound walls have been recorded for at least five other sites in the Globe vicinity (Wilcox, Robertson, and Wood 2001:192).

The only example of what could have been a warrior burial of which I have direct knowledge is that of a tall young man between 18 and 22 years of age who was buried at Pinal Pueblo. The grave was large, 6 by 4 feet, and an unusual 6 feet deep. It was oriented with the head to the north, feet to the south. Steps were cut into the wall of the north end, allowing access to the grave floor. The body was covered with two plaited mats, one over the upper body, and one over the lower body. The offerings included arrows crested with red and blue paint, and a handful of red and blue painted rods resting on his chest. They appeared to be gaming pieces. As recorded in photos given to me by William Underwood, about 20 pottery vessels were arranged around the lower part of the body (Figure 34). Of greatest interest was a gaudy, oval Tonto

Polychrome bowl, with red, black, and white interior decoration. It was the size and shape of half a long watermelon and was placed across the foot of the grave.

At Gila Pueblo, the younger of the presumed Winter Moiety leaders was of an age consistent with his being a warrior. The elder of this group was armed with a small double-bitted axe, which when found in upland Salado sites, Hohmann and others consider it to be a weapon, and thereby associated with warriors. A second double-bitted axe was found in Room 106. At Hagen Site, a double-bitted axe was found in Room 3 (McKusick and Young 1997: 28, 50, 102). At Besh-Ba-Gowah, Patio W.D. 1, Burial 53 was a young adult male with a double-bitted axe in his left hand. He was buried with four turquoise pendants, red pigment, and a corrugated jar, but no polychrome vessels which would provide a relative date. Double-bitted axes from Gila Pueblo and the Hagen site date in the A.D. 1440s.

Other Besh-Ba-Gowah burials present a complex sample. An old adult male was buried with a bone dagger between his ribs. He was buried with discoidal beads around his right wrist, and five vessels; none were polychrome, which may indicate an early interment. Three Besh-Ba-Gowah male burials (112, 123, 198), had arrow points in places that would have caused death. They were accompanied by Gila Polychrome vessels, dating their interments to later than A.D. 1325. Non-perishable offerings numbered one, four, and seventeen. The "Twin Burial" consists of a burial of two children, six to seven years old, which Vickrey interpreted as having been executed. Robert McKusick recalls that each exhibited a linear, vertical hole in the skull, a little left of center, which is more suggestive of a right-handed blow struck with a small, double-bitted axe, than of being shot with an arrow. This burial was accompanied by a Tonto Polychrome beaker-shaped jar, indicating a late interment. All six of these persons appear to have been victims of attack. The old man and the young children can probably be eliminated from consideration as warriors. The other three are probable warriors. These wounds on these individuals, shot in the back, or struck in the head, sometimes from behind, compare well with the victims of the last attack on Gila Pueblo.

Bone daggers were found with male burials 5a and 99; the first with four pre-polychrome vessels, and the second with nine offerings, including Pinto Polychrome and Pinto Black-on-red vessels, and were early. In addition to a bone dagger, a female burial, 64, had two bowls, Gila and Tonto Polychromes, and was late in the occupation.

Burial 90a in Patio Y, a young adult male, had a white spear point lying parallel with the leg bones. Among the seven vessels included in the burial were a Fourmile Polychrome jar and a Gila Polychrome bowl. Burial 91a, Patio Y, a young adult male with a total of 16 groups of offerings, may have held a position similar to that of a Gila Pueblo moiety leader. A bone implement with turquoise inlays, a flint arrow point, and a *Haliotis* shell ornament, found at the back of his skull, appears to be an elaborately decorated hairpin. A large obsidian spear point lay centered above his pelvis, as well as green and red paint which "is on bark and perhaps some buckskin" covering his upper legs may indicate a shield. Offerings included Gila Polychrome vessels, a mass of *Olivella* shell beads above the knees, 60 *Conus* shell tinklers in a mass of green pigment near the right tibia, and small discoidal stone beads around the left tibia. The grave was cribbed transversely with wood.

Based on these burials, I have no doubts that the Upland Salados had warriors throughout their history. The question that remains is whether or not they had a Warrior Society. The dated raids on Gila Pueblo occurred at ca. A.D. 1260, ca. 1340, and ca. 1440. If raids occurred that infrequently, would there have been a practical need for a warrior society? Perhaps a Warrior Society existed as a defensive deterrent, much like a National Guard. After all, the population at the end of this period was concentrated in settlement clusters with a no man's land between them (Wilcox, Robertson, and Wood 2001: 166; Wilcox, Gregory, and Hill 2009:177, 191). If there was no Warrior Society, or at least an Age Stage Warrior Organization, could a settlement cluster have maintained its territory? Probably they could not.

Membership in a Warrior Society could have served the society as a whole, and extended between a youth's second initiation and the time when he married and had a family to care for. Almost certainly a Warrior Society would have involved religious duties in conjunction with the Women's Society, which promoted the fertility and/or renewal of mankind and game, and promoted corn production. These religious duties would have been a continuation in some form of the Ce Àcatl/Morning Star Warrior and the beautiful adolescent water goddess Chalchihuitlicue/Our Lady of the Turquoise Skirt copulating couple fertility concept (Figure 37). This motif occurs early in Hohokam red-on-buff and Mimbres B/w pottery (Moulard 1981: Plates 57, 8, and 9). Locally, it appears in the petroglyphs upstream from Government Springs Ranch in the Dripping Springs drainage. These petroglyphs appear to range in age from Archaic to Apache.

Today, the Morning Star Warrior and Lady Precious Green appear in local Roman Catholic churches, and in local private homes, as St. Michael the Archangel, and as Our Lady of Guadalupe. St. Michael is currently considered a protector from "the Devil and all his works." Our Lady of Guadalupe is currently considered a protector who rescues the innocent from unexpected catastrophe and protects the unborn. Her image is often the larger of the two.

The large, second story of Room 110 at Gila Pueblo, with its arrow shaft straighteners, seems to have served as a general men's meeting room. Both a Hunting Society and a Warrior Society could have met there. An antlered deer cranium, crushed when the roof fell, may be part of a deer dancer headpiece which was hung from the rafters. Room 110 had a roof with a ramada above, which could have represented the Upper World, a second-story men's room which could have represented the Middle World, and a ground-floor ceremonial room with limited access, which could have represented the Lower World. The second-story men's meeting room had a foot-square aperture in its floor through which could be viewed the altar pieces and the slat altar in the ceremonial room beneath. It would have been an ideal site for the initiation of children who were at last allowed to view representations of the sacred.

Cotton-growing and Male Weaving Specialists

Originally, Gila Pueblo ground-floor ceremonial Room 110 had two looms for weaving narrow cloth. During the A.D. 1345 reconstruction, two more looms were installed on the opposite wall. These four looms were of a size suitable for the production of men's loincloths. A Mimbres bowl design shows a loom of this type provided with a movable stool or bench which could be hung up out of the way when the room was in ceremonial use (Moulard 1981: Plate 3).

A marked contrast to these looms is a larger blanket-sized loom installation in Gila Pueblo, Room 104. It is marked by a broad, rectangular area of layers of plaited matting, apparently an attempt to prevent or ameliorate "weaver's bottom," a painful affliction of the ischium (Martin 2000: 281). This padding was layered from the time the room was built, before A.D. 1340, until the 1440s, when the pueblo was destroyed. Canyon Creek Ruin (Haury 1934: 88-89, 91, Plate LIX) contained a long-staple cotton blanket, 39 × 50 inches, with a transverse warp which could have been made on this type of loom. Running the warp transversely would have taken a little longer to set up the loom, but would have been a great saving in weaving time, because it requires many fewer casts of the shuttle. This loom would have been used by several generations, which may imply a family specialty rather than a trade organization.

Aside from raw material for weaving, cotton was present in large quantity at the time of the 1440s destruction. Second-story Room 111 of the ceremonial/redistribution complex contained a very large quantity of cotton in the boll, remaining from the previous year's crop, since the crop of the year of the destruction would not have been mature yet. This large scale storage of cotton suggests some involvement of a group larger than the family in the accumulation, storage, and disbursal of this valuable commodity. Cotton in the boll could have been traded, but finished cloth would have been a greater value per pound, and is easier to transport.

Male Shellworking Specialists

Laevicardium shell was imported from the Gulf of California/Sea of Cortez, and made into commercial lengths of fine shell beads at Besh-Ba-Gowah, Pinal Pueblo, and Gila Pueblo, as indicated by unworked shell, large quantities of finished product, and the presence of debitage, and large quantities of broken shell, especially near the beak, which was unsuitable for jewelry production (Boggess, Ajeman, Gilman, and Bozarth 1992: 188). Considering the complexities of obtaining the raw materials, and of distributing the finished product, a formal organization of this craft specialty is possible.

Deep Ceremonial Room 16 at Besh-Ba-Gowah was surrounded on the south and east by a series of six small, ground-level rooms. The largest of these served as a backstage room for Room 16 and was connected to it by an aperture and echo chamber which could have provided drumming or blowing smoke, to enhance dramatic presentations for an audience in Room 16. This tiny backstage room had four pits, and was connected to an even smaller storage room to the south. Four other storage rooms do not have any surviving floor-level doorways, and may have been accessed through raised doorways (Hohmann, Germick, and Adams 1992:92-102). Hohmann's group suggested that these rooms may have been used to protect costly raw materials and even more costly finished goods like shell jewelry and turquoise. If this model is relevant, some organization larger than family craftsmen would have been involved.

Gila Pueblo shell plays a prominent role in Bradley's study of Casas Grandes Trade Network shell exchange (Bradley 1999). The boundary of the Casas Grandes marine shell trade extends north from Casas Grandes through Alamogordo and Gran Quivira to Pecos, southwest to Allentown and the VIV Ruin, and southeast through Besh-Ba-Gowah and Gila Pueblo, then south and east of the Santa Cruz River, to include Babocomari, and Slaughter Ranch. The boundary then proceeds southeast back to the Casas Grandes area. The Hohokam Marine Shell Network extends in an arc on the west, beginning at Tres Alamos, and including Casa Grande, Los Muertos, Tonto Cliff Dwellings, Tuzigoot, Wupatki, and Awatovi, ending at Chaco Canyon on the east, and Aztec on the north. The sources of marine shell, the places of shell manufacture, and the markets for shell jewelry are different for each marine shell trade network. Shell artifact totals in Bradley's Table 16-1 (Bradley 1999: p. 216) for Gila Pueblo proper obviously do not include the numbers for the 1970s excavation, which yielded 240 individual shell artifacts, plus a stomacher containing 6-7,000 beads. Added to Bradley's total for Gila Pueblo shell artifacts from previous excavations, the sum is 11,764 artifacts, plus the 6–7000-bead stomacher. This total compares well with a total of 15,458 for Grasshopper, and a total of 36,898 for Casas Grandes, the center from which marine shell was disbursed into this network. When the projected population of Gila Pueblo is calculated using the 1.6–2 person per room ratio employed by Wilcox, Robertson, and Wood (1999: p 163, Table 7.3), the projected population of Gila Pueblo proper is 320–400.   This same table lists the population of Grasshopper as 2,766-3,458 in later Pueblo IV. The number of shell artifacts per resident is so high at Gila Pueblo that shell working is a conspicuous cultural focus at that site.

Female Pigment-Grinding Specialists

The second-story Room 105 at Gila Pueblo and the roof above it were involved in the grinding of pigments in commercial quantities. This activity appears to have been carried out by women (see discussion of Burial 192, below). The roof was provided with small metates so several different pigments could be ground at the same time. The pigments produced included blue azurite, and green malachite, both copper compounds; red, yellow, and black iron oxides; and white selenite. The finished product, finely ground colored powder, was recovered in small jars and folded up in scraps of plain-weave cotton rag, though other containers could have been used. Red iron oxide powder was more common, in quantities of a double handful; malachite was found in smaller quantity, a small handful. The powder sprinkled over burials at Besh-Ba-Gowah was in considerably larger quantity, and could be considered conspicuous consumption.

Burial 192, North Patio, Besh-Ba-Gowah, contained a 21- to 25-year-old woman buried with a mano and a metate containing green pigment. Painted pottery from the grave included San Carlos Red-on-brown, Pinto Polychrome, and Gila Polychrome, which places the date of the burial somewhere around A.D. 1300-1325. Quantities of pigment in this and other burials suggest that commercial production of pigments was present at least as early as Burial 192. Hohmann (1992a: 543) states that over 34 percent of Besh-Ba-Gowah burials had bodies covered with red ochre, and about 1.7 percent had bodies covered with green malachite or blue azurite.

8—Religious Change at Gila Pueblo

The Ceremonial/Redistribution Complex

The excavation of the ceremonial/redistribution complex at Gila Pueblo took place in the 1970s as part of classes I taught for Gila Pueblo College. The students set the research goals and their main interest was in testing Gladwin's claim that the pueblo had been attacked and burned. Another interest was to watch for any sign of Mesoamerican influence. Working from the known to the unknown, we ran a trench across the south end of Gladwin's excavation to discover walls, estimate the amount of earth to be moved, and set up a plan of excavation achievable by the end of each semester.

The fact that we ended up in a ceremonial/redistribution complex was a happy accident; one that yielded many discoveries. Among them:

- We found that Gladwin was right; the pueblo had been attacked and burned in the 1400s. We dug deeper than Gladwin had, all the way to sterile ground, and found two earlier fires and a Paleo-Indian campsite.

- We learned that a Ramos Polychrome effigy jar had been recovered from Besh-Ba-Gowah. That, and my identification of two macaws that had been included in a high-status burial at Pinal Pueblo, were both indicators of Mesoamerican contact.

- We were surprised to find such a large quantity of shell, both worked and unworked, as well as species of shell that placed Gila Pueblo firmly in the Casas Grande Shell Trade Network.

- We were also surprised to find icons of such Mesoamerican supernaturals as Xiuhtecutli, Tlaloc, Chalchihuitlicue, and various avatars of Quetzalcoatl in artifacts and pottery design.

- Finding elaborately costumed high-status personages, valuable imports from distant places, and valuable trade export goods in the form of turquoise jewelry, fine shell beads, powdered pigments, and finely woven cotton cloth, in addition to the expected Salado Polychromes were also surprises. Bones of a Tularosa Turkey recovered from a cache pit in a Women's Society room led to research culminating in my book, *Southwest Birds of Sacrifice*. A stone pipe recovered by Alan Ferg, and paintings of horn worms, hawk moths, and Datura pods on polychrome pottery led to the sections on iconography and hallucinogens herein. Foci of ceremonial activity and locations of religious artifact are pictured for each stage of the occupation of Gila Pueblo in Figure 28, as are evidences of closing activities.

The ceremonial/redistribution complex at Gila Pueblo brought a large, diverse, and well-dated group of data together in one place, enabling us to observe continuities and changes through a period of more than 200 years. It was a community center where important things happened. The Upland Salados were not simple hillbillies carrying on a marginal subsistence in a remote, quiet backwater, as they had been considered in the past. The Upland Salados were part of a vibrant, vigorous trade network with far-flung influences.

The excavation of Gila Pueblo is not over. A large portion of the rooms attached to the ceremonial/redistribution complex have been saved. They are there for the day when new methods are available and new questions need to be answered.

The Early Postclassic International Symbol Set

The Salado religious outlook is inseparable from the duality of the shaman/patron of hunters and the midwife/patron of game animals concept brought from the Old World by the earliest inhabitants of the Southwest (see Chapter 1). However, by the late Archaic, Maya cosmology and iconography had begun to spread along trade routes in a form Boone and Smith (2003: 189) call the Early Postclassic International Set. This iconography was present in the pottery decoration of the Mimbres Valley, and after the ending of the Mimbres Classic Period, ca. A.D. 1150, the same iconography continues in White Mountain Red Ware, in such motifs as the morning and evening star, snakes, hawk moths, and sunflowers; and in the painted pottery of the local Salado Pueblos. This iconography expresses a concept of four directions defining the four quarters of the visible world, of zenith (above), nadir (below) and center, where all axes intersect. The sun is visualized as passing into the underworld in the west, lighting the dwelling place of the dead when it is night in the world above, and reemerging to light the land of the living when dawn breaks in the east. Like night and day, the seasons are reversed: when it is summer in the visible world, it is winter in the underworld, and vice versa.

When the sun sets or a person dies, their entry to the underworld is troubled by monsters, which the sun, or the dead, must pass before they can proceed. One of these monsters was known by its Uto-Aztecan day name, which translates as "Seven Macaw." The Mimbres painted this monster in the process of being slain by the Hero Twins, as an enormous seven-week-old macaw, that stage at which it must be taken from its nest in the wild and hand raised if it is to become tame, that is, human-imprinted, and to have commercial value (Figure 31). A" bronco" macaw, one that is not human-imprinted, is a vicious monster which is dangerous and cannot be successfully kept in captivity. This is a visual record of a verbal pun, "Seven Macaw," suggesting that Uto-Aztecan was understood by the artist.

Other events, which could be equated with sunset or death, but which are not regularly observed, are eclipses. In one illustration of a lunar eclipse, a giant bat, with a Xolotl/Younger Brother/sun-going-down cross on its wing, and a moon rabbit in its paws, bears the darkened moon encircled by its tail. Another lunar eclipse motif depicts a giant snake monster, bulging because it has swallowed the moon whole, like a bull snake swallows an egg whole (Figure 31).

Since Mimbres pictorial pottery went out of style ca. A.D. 1150, and the local Salado pueblos began to be built 75 years later, it is reasonable to suppose that ideas expressed in Mimbres and White Mountain Red Ware pottery designs prevailed into the Salado period.

Date	Event
1225	Gila Pueblo and Besh-Ba-Gowah constructed.
1260	First destruction of Gila Pueblo by fire caused by attackers from the Armer Ranch area.
1340	Earthquake and, immediately after, destruction of Gila Pueblo by fire caused by attackers from a neighboring pueblo, probably Besh-Ba-Gowah.
1345	Gila pueblo reoccupied, probably by people from small settlements in nearby foothills.
1385	Major renovation.
1440s	Depopulation of Gila Pueblo by attackers from the Armer Ranch area. Closing activities and burning of pueblo by survivors.

Table 5. Gila Pueblo Timeline (all dates approximate)

Religion at the Time of the ca. A.D. 1260 Destruction

In A.D. 1260, Gila Pueblo was a multi-roomed pueblo surrounded by an area of ridgetop smaller settlements, whose inhabitants were farming the canyon bottoms with the aid of ditch irrigation. The east-west orientation of Gila Pueblo's entry and paired patios, and the north-south orientation of Besh-Ba-Gowah's entry and paired patios, suggest that the pueblos worked in complementary duality, in the sponsorship of the four main solar observances. Gila Pueblo probably hosted equinox festivals, and Besh-Ba-Gowah probably hosted solstice festivals. It is likely that these occasions served the entire vicinity, since there are no signs of neighboring ceremonial centers. Hohokam ritual items, such as censers and palettes, continued in use throughout the Salado occupation.

The first destruction of Gila Pueblo, dated at ca. A.D. 1260 by radiocarbon and archaeomagnetic methods and roughly 80 years before the earthquake-and-attack destruction discussed earlier, resulted in the burning of both stories of the ceremonial/redistribution complex. None of the plaster on the walls or floor was washed away by exposure to rain, indicating that the structure was re-roofed immediately. The only signs in the ground-floor ceremonial Room 110 (there were two stories topped by a ramada) of the catastrophe were ash and a thin, triangular arrow point beautifully flaked from fine-grain chert matching those from the Armer Ranch Site on the Salt River, embedded in the crack between the wall plaster and the floor plaster (Figure 30). In A.D. 1260, the ceremonial/redistribution complex consisted of four second-story rooms, and more than eight ground-floor rooms, a total of more than 12 rooms. At this point there were doorways leading from Room 110 to Room 111 on the south, to an unknown number of rooms on the west, at least two rooms on the north, and a centrally located floor-level aperture on the east wall, which was filled throughout the duration of the occupation with a permanent slat altar, illuminated by a small, raised fireplace (McKusick and Young 1997: pp. 19, 21, 24). Room 110 was empty. The only foci of ceremonial activity at the time of the A.D. 1260 burning were the slat altar in Room 110, and a beautiful, non-utilitarian greenstone axe on the floor of Room 111. A total of 10 greenstone axes were recovered on or beneath the room floors of the NAN Ranch Ruin, which lies in the Mimbres Valley of New Mexico.

Figure 31. Mimbres Depictions of Monsters. <u>Top</u>: Monster Seven Macaw slain by Younger Brother; Nesbitt-Logan Museum Collection, after Davis 1995: 195. <u>Middle</u>: lunar eclipse, Bat Monster encircling darkened moon with Xolotl/Younger Brother/sun-going-down cross on its wing and moon rabbit in its paws; Nesbitt-Logan Museum Collection, after Davis 1995: 195. <u>Bottom</u>: lunar eclipse, moon swallowed by a snake monster, sun in Underworld circled by snake tail, after Moulard 1981: Plate 21.

Evidence from this site suggests that greenstone axes may have been used in both beginning new construction and in closing ceremonies, and that they may have been viewed as "lineage" property with "as much symbolic as functional importance" (Shafer 2003: 200-201). The NAN Ranch Site also had Mimbres III pottery vessels (Shafer 2003:245) which appear to be precursors of Cliff Polychrome.

Room 105 to the east was the backstage room for the slat altar, and had doorways to two rooms on the east wall and to Room 101 on the south. Ground-floor Room 105 was entered by climbing down a ladder from the second-story roof to the second-story floor of Room 101, thence down another ladder to the ground floor of Room 101, and passing through a doorway in the north wall to Room 105. From this restricted access room, puppetry, sound effects, musical accompaniment, and perhaps clouds of smoke, could be made to appear in Room 110 (Figure 28).

It was the opinion of White Bear Fredericks that puppet-like effigies were manipulated through apertures in the slat altar, which may have had hinged covers, to illustrate dramatic presentations concerning creation myths and other subjects. He suggested that a flexible water serpent effigy (First Mesa Paalölöqangwlalwa, "Water Serpent" Dance, Stephen 1936: 287-307) could have been shot forth through such an aperture using "lightning sticks." These are a series of sticks fastened together by their ends and crossed centers in a multiple X formation. There are two handles on one end, and a prong to which an effigy may be attached on the other. When the handles are spread, the lightning sticks fold back; when the handles are squeezed together, the lightning sticks scissor forward. This simple device can move an effigy backwards and forwards, as well as moving it from side to side, and up or down. Use in historic times of a lightning lattice, or frame, or "house," or "snake" of this sort is documented for Hopi, Zuni, Acoma, Cochiti, and Zia (Parsons 1939: 378; Stephen 1936: 308–309, figure 182; White 1962: 319), and is believed to be present among the wooden ritual artifacts recovered from Chetro Ketl, Chaco Canyon, New Mexico, dating to around A.D. 1100 (Vivian, Dodgen, and Hartmann 1978: 54-55, 110). Historic puppet-like plumed serpent effigies or "mask-images" have been described and illustrated for Hopi and Zuni (Stephen 1936: 305-307; Stevenson 1904: 94-102).

Adjoining this central unit on the south were dwelling Room 103 and its storeroom, Room 108. Following the ca. A.D. 1260 destruction, the hearth of Room 103 was closed, never to be used again. Room 100, to the east, with its floor-level door and adjoining portal appears, from accumulated garbage, to have been used for processing small game like hares and rabbits. After the A.D. 1260 attack, during which the portal was burned, exterior doorways were eliminated, as were ground-level ramadas. The roof tops were bordered by knee-high balustrades, and the ramada work areas were moved to the roofs.

Religion at the Time of the ca. A.D. 1325 Expansion

Shortly after A.D. 1325, Room 99, complete with a rectangular hearth and *piki* stone resting upon three fire dogs, and Room 102 were built on top of the burned roof supports of the old portal (Figure 28, lower-left). Dating is based on the subfloor presence of Fourmile Polychrome, which began to be manufactured about A.D. 1325, and Pinto Polychrome, which ceased to be manufactured at about the same time. This same deposit contained the bulbous neck portion of what appeared to be a small Gila Polychrome datura brewing or storage jar, shaped like a small bottle gourd. Datura use is likely as early in the Southwest as there were humans present to use it. However, the early Gila Polychrome jar fragment, dating ca. A.D. 1325, is the first indication of datura use at Gila Pueblo. Evidences of religious activity remaining from this time period are the slat altar and the datura jar (Figure 28, lower-left).

Between A.D. 1325 and 1340, a complex of four rooms (Rooms 98, 104, 109, and an unexcavated room) was added to the southeast corner of Gila Pueblo. The south and west walls are of unsupported adobe. The north wall, informally constructed of a little stone, horizontal sticks, and abundant adobe, was originally a compound wall. Shiner's Room 97, to the north, appears to have been a partitioned passageway between the roomblock and the compound wall.

Religion at the Time of the ca. A.D. 1340 Destruction

The destruction of Gila Pueblo ca. A.D. 1340, first by earthquake and then by attackers using local projectile points was sudden, catastrophic, and opportunistic. The earthquake was so severe that it brought the walls of Gila Pueblo down lower in a few moments than have the centuries succeeding the pueblo's last occupation. This disaster had three contributing causes. First, the very active Miami Fault, the action of which produced unusually durable pottery clay, veins of kaolin for white slip, and a variety of colorful metallic oxides which were an important Salado commercial commodity, moves constantly. The daily blasting at the local mines make this happen a little at a time, for the most part, but even so we wake up some mornings to find locked doors sprung open, and pictures hanging on the walls at odd angles. Without the ameliorating action of blasting, prehistoric earthquakes would have been less frequent, but more violent.

If my scenario about friction between Gila Pueblo and Besh-Ba-Gowah is correct, the second probable cause of the ca. A.D. 1340 destruction of Gila Pueblo lay in the geography of Six Shooter Canyon. Gila Pueblo lies above a broad flat area in the canyon which could accommodate expansive irrigated fields. Besh-Ba-Gowah and Pinal Pueblo, just over 1 mile downstream, are in a narrower part of the canyon, and have less room for fields close to the pueblos. Success in corn production is dependent upon having enough water for pollen production while the corn is producing tassels. If the inhabitants of Gila Pueblo had diverted too much irrigation water when the corn was tasseling, their children might have been well fed, while the children at Besh-Ba-Gowah might have starved. This situation would not have made for good feelings among neighbors.

Third, the early A.D. 1300s was a time of high precipitation in the central mountains of Arizona, but precipitation decreased markedly about 1340 (Crary, Germick, and Golio 1994: 58-59). Times had been good, trade had flourished, and the population had expanded. A sudden and persistent period of drought would have been an added stressor.

When the earthquake struck, Gila Pueblo was devastated. Those trying to free the trapped were killed by attackers, probably from Besh-Ba-Gowah, firing thick side-notched projectile points of local manufacture (Figure 30), and the pueblo was set ablaze with the dead, dying, and trapped consumed in the conflagration. The pueblo stood empty for at least five years, judging from the depth of wall plaster that washed down and covered the bones and wreckage lying within the broken walls. This estimate of the length of time the ruin stood open is based on measurement of loss of plaster after the excavation was terminated by a change in college administration.

The period preceding the ca. A.D. 1340 destruction was the flowering of Gila Pueblo's occupation. The ca. A.D. 1260 attack had drastically reduced the population, but the centralized organization persisted, and the room interiors were little changed. Shell was the best in quality and variety. Gila Polychrome pottery, much of which may have been made at Gila Pueblo, was abundant even in the small, neighboring ridgetop sites.

One interesting development was the apparent ownership of the outcrop of Pinal Schist, which lies about two blocks south of Gila Pueblo. Door lintels at Gila Pueblo were made of Pinal Schist. Burials at the Derringer Drive site just across the wash west of Gila Pueblo were cribbed with Pinal Schist. In contrast, door lintels and burial cribbing at Besh-Ba-Gowah were made of wood.

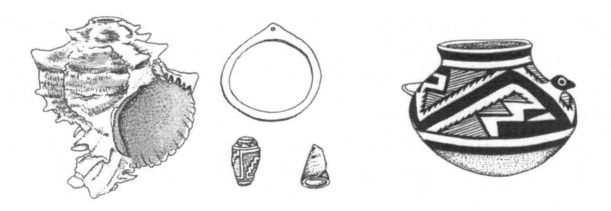

Figure 32. Religious Artifacts ca. A.D. 1340. <u>Left</u>: Princely Murex (Hexiplex brassica), shell trumpet altarpiece, Scale: ×0.5, Room 110, Gila Pueblo. <u>Center-top</u>: Glycymeris maculata earring. <u>Center-bottom-left</u>: a carved Oliva shell bead. <u>Center-bottom-right</u>: Conus shell tinkler, Scale: all ×0.5. <u>Right</u>: Gila Polychrome quail effigy jar, located behind slat altar, in Room 105, Gila Pueblo.

Religious artifacts in Room 110 at the time of the earthquake (Figure 32) include a Princely Murex, *Hexiplex brassica,* trumpet which lay with the embrasure directed toward the slat altar, a carved olive shell, *Oliva* sp., and two small *Glycymeris* earrings, *Glycymeris maculata,* which were attached to, or hanging from, the north edge of the slat altar. An intact Gila Polychrome quail effigy lay in the wreckage of Room 105, behind the slat altar. Again, the slat altar is the primary focus of religious activity.

Evidence of one sodality survives from the ca. A.D. 1340 destruction in the form of the large adult male who died, in the west doorway of Room 110. He appeared to be wearing hunter's brush chaps fastened with *Conus* shell tinklers used as toggles.

Religion at the Time of the ca. A.D. 1345 Reoccupation

Assuming that the population of Gila Pueblo was exterminated in ca. A.D. 1340, or that a few survivors were absorbed into other pueblos, as was the case in the destruction of Awatovi (Brooks 2016), the question arises of who rebuilt Gila Pueblo. The predominant decorated pottery at the small sites on the ridges in the area was Gila Polychrome, and the new settlers made and used Gila Polychrome. The lack of rainfall and the threat of attack had both become problems. The most likely answer to the question of the identity of the new inhabitants of Gila Pueblo is that they were local farmers who gathered together at this period to take advantage of a vacant but repairable pueblo which would provide them mutual protection. The canyons continued to be farmed, but the hilltop pueblos seem to have been deserted at this time, since they lack sherds identifiable as Tonto Polychrome or as Cliff Polychrome. This reoccupation is tree-ring dated at ca. A.D. 1345.

If a model is to be considered which involves the reoccupation of Gila Pueblo by the inhabitants of numerous small ridgetop pueblos, the question arises of how they might have governed themselves. The dual division of architecture at both Gila Pueblo and at Besh-Ba-Gowah extends from ca. A.D. 1225 to the 1440s. If Gila Pueblo and Besh-Ba-Gowah had alternated in serving the surrounding settlements with important solar festivals, the lack of one set would have been a serious disruption of the yearly ceremonial calendar. A conglomeration of slightly different groups, which previously had been served by Gila Pueblo ceremonial leadership for important festivals, would have had the general knowledge, if not all the songs and paraphernalia, to reestablish the pueblo as a functioning, but slightly different, ceremonial partner to Besh-Ba-Gowah.

Many years ago, when I was considering the differing faunal usage of the groups at Grasshopper Pueblo living on opposite sides of the Salt River Wash, I remarked to White Bear that anthropologists considered Zuni to have moieties, whereas Hopis had phratries, multiple groups of related clans. He looked at me in open-mouthed astonishment. "But," he exclaimed, "when the time comes to tell all the stories, we sit down in two groups, facing each other, and we all listen to be sure that every word is correct." Apparently Native American viewpoints do not always fit anthropological theory as well as we believe.

Bernardini (2011: 196-220) considers the problem of religion and agglomeration among the Hopi. He divides the agglomerating groups into early local populations, the Motisinom; and later populations, the Nùutungkwisinom, coming in from more distant areas. In general, the earlier settlers appear to control katsina ceremonies, while the latecomers appear to control non-katsina ceremonies. The Hopi ceremonial calendar is divided into two separate halves. The katsina ceremonial season is controlled by the Motisinom, and is, at least at present, "democratic, public, and benign" (Bernardini 2011: 205). Both the participants and the audience have access to katsina ritual. In contrast, the non-katsina rituals of the Nùutungkwisinom societies are the closely held property of controlling clans, require initiation to perform, and are often private, and "restrictive, esoteric, and dangerously powerful," (Bernardini 2011: 206). This division, which works like a moiety system, at least in White Bear's mind, is actually a division between ancient local lineages, and more recent sodalities controlled by incoming clans.

110

Perhaps, like their better known neighbors to the north, the new inhabitants of Gila Pueblo muddled along as best they could, settling in a pueblo which was already in dual-division layout. Room 110, which appears to have been used alternately by the dual halves of the pueblo in its earlier days, is now divided, visually at least, into two halves, which could have been used simultaneously by both halves of the pueblo. This situation continues throughout the remaining years of the pueblo.

If we accept this model of an agglomerated society, we are left with a working pueblo on the one hand, but with surplus leadership on the other. Sodalities are supposed to function as integrating agents which crosscut lineage structures. Perhaps these natural leaders put their organizational talents to work in sodalities which both served and unified the pueblo, and in time resulted in the formation of warrior, hunting, and women's societies, and trade specialists.

Gila Pueblo was rebuilt by people with the same needs as the original inhabitants, but with slight variations to the original plan. Crowding is apparent. Doorways were blocked to provide more living units. Room 110 went from three doorways to one, and had only three adjoining rooms. Room 105 went from three doorways to one, and adjoined only Room 101, its original means of entry. Room 103 was separated from Room 108, and Room 99 was separated from Room 100, but retained Storeroom 102. The four-room adobe suite on the southeast corner of the pueblo was divided into two separate living room and storage room units.

Part of the reason for doorway blockage was the presence in the west doorway of Room 110 of the burned body of a high-status man, and in the doorway between Rooms 99 and 100 of the burned body of a younger man, both trapped by the earthquake, and killed in the ensuing attack and conflagration before they could be rescued. Salados do not appear to have had any dread of old bones. In these cases they simply covered them up with a layer of wall plaster.

Room 110, which was originally a single unit, now had two sipapus, one in the center of the north half, and one in the center of the south half, effectively dividing the room into two use areas. Two looms were built to cover the plastered-over west doorway, which also balanced the looms which filled the space on the east wall between the centrally located slat altar and the north wall. The ceremonial/redistribution complex contracted from more than 12 rooms to only six.

During this period, three raised cobble-and-adobe platforms were constructed in Room 105 to serve as bases for large basketry granaries (Figure 33). Presumably, these large storage units were used to provide supplies for community wide feasting upon important occasions. Granary platforms of this type are found in southern Chihuahua, Mexico, extending north along the Rio Papigochi, Rio Sirupa, Rio Chico, and Rio Piedra Verdes to Paquimé, and thence to the San Pedro, Dripping Springs Wash, Pinal Creek, Salt River, and Tonto Creek (Fisher 2003; Lindauer 1996: pp. 841-859).

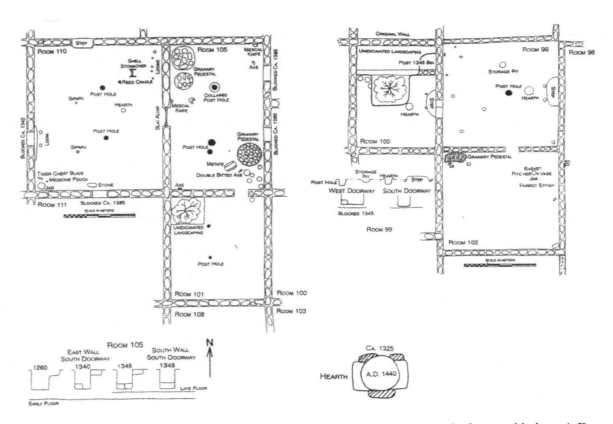

Figure 33. Gila Pueblo Granary Platforms. <u>Top and bottom-left</u>: Room 105, platforms added ca. A.D. 1345. <u>Right</u>: Room 102, platform added ca. A.D. 1385. <u>Bottom-center</u>: Room 99 hearth detail, before and after removal of piki stone, ca. A.D. 1385.

The Piki Stone Is Broken: The ca. A.D. 1385 Renovation

A major period of renovation is tree-ring dated at ca. A.D. 1385. A granary pedestal was added to Room 102. The south door of Room 110 was blocked, reducing the ceremonial/redistribution complex room count to five. Sometime between A.D. 1385 and 1440, two new rooms were attached to the south end of the pueblo, Room 106 and Room 107. Each of these rooms had low, informally constructed walls made of large boulders which formed the base of a jacal superstructure. Room 97, excavated by Joel Shiner (1961: 6, Figure 2), appears to have been converted to ceremonial use at this time. The room was apparently originally a passageway between the pueblo and the compound wall. Shiner dug for six and a half meters without finding the masonry end wall he expected. The room may have been extraordinarily long, or may have been partitioned with jacal, which was unexpected and therefore unrecognized.

At some point after the A.D. 1385 renovation, hearths became deeper and were edged with a raised ring of adobe which supported large Cliff Polychrome cooking bowls manufactured from about A.D. 1350 to about 1450. The bulging sides of these 33-35 cm bowls were presumably harnessed with rawhide, to which were affixed two wooden handles, for ease of lifting, just like an historic Zuni bowl which is in the collection of the Heard Museum (Figure 34, lower-right). A small bed of glowing coals in the bottom of the hearth warmed this slow-cooker. Small corrugated cooking jars were found propped on ash pits at floor level next to the hearth.

There has been considerable discussion over many years about the purpose of corrugated pottery. From the corrugated ware found in use at the fall of Gila Pueblo, it is apparent that large corrugated jars were put in place in store rooms, and never moved again. They were really too heavy to move. In this case, the corrugation gave a large exterior surface, from which moisture could evaporate, to help keep the contents of the sealed jar dry. Smaller jars, which were easily portable, were used for cooking. In this case, the large exterior surface helped absorb radiant heat from the coals of the ash pit upon which they were propped.

A major change in religious observance was the introduction of the burial of infants under the floors of the ceremonial/redistribution complex, and Shiner's Room 97. Shiner's excavation uncovered four infant burials, one of which was accompanied by a cloth-wrapped copper bell. This is the earliest dated bell recorded for Gila Pueblo. There may have been infant burials beneath residential-room floors earlier, but there were none in the ceremonial/ redistribution complex before 1385.

Eight additional infant burials were recovered from beneath the ceremonial/redistribution complex. The most elaborate of these was Burial 11, located in Room 105, just within the doorway. It contained a four- or five-month-old fetus buried in a vault made of golf ball-sized spheres about 5 cm in diameter, deliberately worked from Schultz Granite. The tiny fetus was enclosed between the halves of a deliberately broken San Carlos Red-on-brown bowl, and was accompanied by fine argillite beads totaling about 70 ml in volume. The beads were made of the brilliant red argillite from the Prescott area, not the local, more brownish argillite (McKusick and Young 1997: 6, 24, 93-96).

Perhaps even more important to the interpretation of this period was Burial 9, Room 101, the access to Room 105. This grave was boot-shaped, a vertical shaft with a side excavation at the bottom so an infant in a cradle board could be laid flat. The bottom of the shaft was floored with the two halves of a deliberately broken *piki* stone, which appears to have rested upon fire dogs in the original rectangular hearth of Room 99, from ca. A.D. 1325 when it was built, to the ca. 1385 renovation. Perishable offerings were placed in the shaft, along with a handsome petrified wood knife (McKusick and Young 1997: 24, 93-96).

The deliberate breaking of this particular *piki* stone may cast some light on the socio/politico/religious change which was taking place. The production of *piki* is a festival activity still carried on in the Hopi pueblos. Following this event, Room 99, which had been an important adjunct to the ceremonial/redistribution complex, became a simple residential room, devoid of ceremonial artifacts, until the end of the occupation.

Figure 34. Tonto/Gila and Cliff Polychrome from Pinal Pueblo. Excavated by William Underwood. <u>Top-left</u> and <u>center-right</u>: two views of a Tonto/Gila Polychrome bowl (ASM catalog # 82-45-40). <u>Bottom-left</u>: Cliff Polychrome bowl (ASM catalog # 82-45-41). Courtesy of Mike Jacobs, Arizona State Museum. <u>Bottom-right</u>: probable method of harnessing, after historic Zuni bowl in Heard Museum collection.

Ceremonial Artifacts at the Time of the A.D. 1440s Destruction

Ceremonial artifacts worn, or carried, by the persons of high-status at the time of the destruction of Gila Pueblo are discussed in the sections on "Costumes."

From the founding of Gila Pueblo until ca. A.D. 1340, when it was destroyed by earthquake and local attack, the ceremonial/redistribution complex had had only one focus, the slat altar. Following the ca. A.D. 1345 reconstruction by a different Salado group, or groups, the ceremonial redistribution complex had three foci, the two sipapus and the slat altar, plus the opposed looms on the east and west walls. By the ca. A.D. 1440s destruction of Gila Pueblo, ceremonial artifacts were widespread throughout the excavated area, a change probably caused by each lineage bringing religious artifacts from their old homes to their new lodgings and/or the formation of sodalities. These artifacts, listed by the room in which they were found, include:

Shiner's Room 97: *Laevicardium* valve painted with azurite (Figure 35) (McKusick and Young 1997: 82).

Room 98: Finds included a storage pit containing the neck bones of a Small Indian Domestic Turkey; a bowling ball-sized greenstone sphere resting on the floor near the north wall; and an oval-shaped Tonto Polychrome bowl, with red, white, and black interior, resting on the floor along the east wall (McKusick and Young 1997: 7, 27). I believe such large, long oval bowls were used as water drums (see discussion in "Flower World" section).

Room 101: The upper story contained fragments of Tonto Polychrome human (Figure 35) and quail effigy jars, and an heirloom saucer made from the side of a St. Johns Polychrome bowl. Quartz crystal fragments were scattered evenly across the ground floor, and a 40-cm selenite crystal was leaning against the north wall of the room, next to the doorway to Room 105 (McKusick and Young 1997: 24).

Room 102: An heirloom Gila Polychrome basket-jar with the handle broken off and ground smooth, a Chupadero b/w pitcher, and a Tonto Polychrome vase (Figure 35) were clustered, apart from fragments of a Tonto Polychrome parrot effigy (McKusick and Young 1997: 26).

Room 103: Tonto Polychrome human and quail effigies (Figure 35); a red-line Tonto Polychrome vase filled with juniper ash; a stone bowl; a Gila Polychrome bowl which held an antler tine, a red concretion, and a ball of ash; and a packet of malachite wrapped in white cotton cloth (McKusick and Young 1997: 25).

Room 106: A corrugated jar held limonite. Other artifacts included a *Melongena* shell trumpet (Figure 35), *Glycymeris* shell bracelets, a small *Glycymeris* pendant, and a quartz crystal found with a small double-bitted axe (McKusick and Young 1997: 28).

Room 108: A redware parrot effigy smashed in the hearth (McKusick and Young 1997: 25).

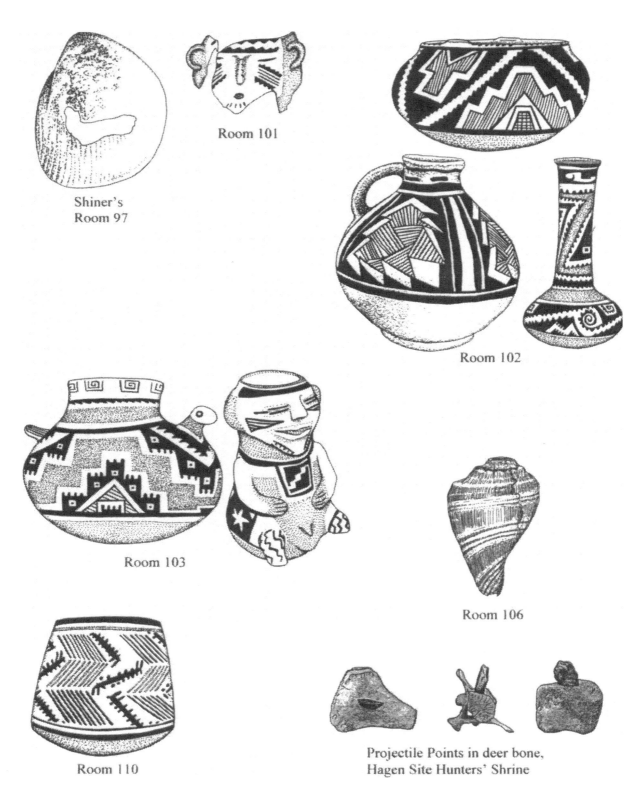

Figure 35. Ceremonial Artifacts at the Time of the A.D. 1440s Destruction of Gila Pueblo.

Room 110: In the center of the upper floor, a plain brownware duck pot with wings, the size of a partially inflated football, was filled with carbonized shelled corn. On the ground floor, a Tonto Polychrome beaker was found, decorated with centipedes and water zigzags (Figure 35) (McKusick and Young 1997: 24).

Room 111: This room was left half-excavated by the termination of the Eastern Arizona College field program, resulting from administrative changes in the Gila Pueblo branch campus. Alan Ferg completed the south half and the sub-A.D. 1440 floor portion of the excavation. The collection was processed at the Arizona State Museum. Draft reports have been prepared on the worked stone (Kim Beckwith and Bruce A. Bradley), botanical specimens (Karen Adams); minerals, pigments, crystals, shell, and bone artifacts (Kim Beckwith); and human bone (Karen K. Zadina) (on file with Alan Ferg, Arizona State Museum). A summary of relevant artifacts is presented here.

The worked bone from Room 111 included a split metapodial hairpin with worked condylar head, and a whole metapodial hairpin (White-tailed Deer, *Odocoileus virginianus*), also with a worked condylar head. A third fragmentary hairpin was made from the proximal portion of a right artiodactyl tibia. A deep groove is incised across the proximal end, and two holes are drilled next to the edge. These hairpins, the hairpins of the high-status men, and a hairpin found in Room 102, were all completely permeated with oil, and had been turned glossy, ebony black by the heat of the fire. The hairpin from Room 102 is considered in this report under "Closing Activities."

Room 111 also yielded a squat, conical, biconically drilled pipe, made from vesicular basalt. There was no dottle in the tube, or evidence of adhesive to attach a mouthpiece (Figure 23). A varied assortment of pigments was found, including prepared red iron oxide slip stored in a small Tonto Polychrome jar. The room contained a large amount of worked and unworked shell, much more than was found on the floors of the remainder of the ceremonial/redistribution complex. An olive green steatite ball-shaped pendant with a stem drilled for suspension appears to be an imitation of a copper bell. Similar pendants, of various stones, have been found at Gila Pueblo, at AZ P:13:7 (ASU) (a Sacaton Phase equivalent site in the Walnut Creek area), Shoofly Ruin, the Sulfur Springs Valley, and two from the Flagstaff area. Since these stone "bells" could not ring, the shape itself might convey the same meaning as a real copper bell, if they were in short supply, or no longer available from the south (Gila Pueblo Room 111 draft report Arizona State Museum Archives).

Like other raw shell found throughout the ca. A.D. 1440s level of the ceremonial/redistribution complex, the shell in Room 111 was dead shell which had been gathered where it was washed up along the beach, rather than shell obtained live by dredging, digging, or diving. This is in sharp contrast to the fine shell from the ca. A.D. 1340 level. This fact, coupled with the presence of imitation bells, suggests a breakdown of the Casas Grandes Trade Network.

Two roughly spherical stone balls were found along the west wall of Room 111. One unmodified quartzite cobble (ASM catalog # 82-45-166) is 6.5 cm in diameter. The other, a minimally modified hematite cobble (ASM catalog # 82-45-165), is 8.3 cm in diameter. Both would have been suitable heads for free-swinging raw-hide-covered club heads like the one carried by the young high-status male killed on the roof over Rooms 99/102.

Religious Iconography in Salado Pottery

In 1981, I had a vivid dream, in brilliant color, of a Pueblo Indian subject which I wished to paint in acrylic as a gift for my husband. I hesitated to do so, for fear of supernatural sanctions, in case the subject had spiritual meaning which would have been inappropriate for me to depict. I told Naomi Bear the content of the dream, and asked her advice. She replied, "You dreamed it. It belongs to you. You can paint it if you want to." I believe this simple answer serves for most Salado pottery motifs. Since potters are assumed to be female, iconography is filtered through their world view. The design local residents call a "bird wing" or "macaw wing," is referred to by Crown as a "feathered serpent" (1994:136). Crown appears to be correct. The running feathered serpent motif is derived from water dogs (Figure 9), which occur in local reservoirs in abundance. Upland Salado macaws, on the other hand, number only two, from a high-status burial at Pinal Pueblo (McKusick 2013: 289).

Tlaloc iconography entered the Southwest as a burial bundle wrapped in a cloud-step blanket, surmounted by a goggle-eyed mask (as in Figure 15) (Schaafsma 2000: p. 65 Figure 7). By the time Besh-Ba-Gowah versions of Tlaloc were depicted in Tonto Polychrome, not much was left but the eyes or only a single eye in negative (Figure 36).

Morning Star and Evening Star Crosses occur frequently. Their distinguishing characteristics are illustrated in Figure 14. Cloud steps may be half, single, or double, and continue in all three forms from beginning to end of the local Salado occupation. Parallel water zigzags, parallel diagonal lines, and descending water squiggles are popular. Figurative designs, such as datura, mountain evening primrose, and horn worms are rare, but Hawk Moths are more common.

Mimbres figurative pottery designs illustrate a local adaptation of iconography common in Mesoamerica. The development of the katsina religion in the Hopi pueblos took this iconography in one direction, and the development of the Salado phenomenon took it in another. Zimmerman (2013: 20-25) considers the sudden appearance of polychrome artistic expression ca. A.D. 1300 from several perspectives. A comparison of an Awatovi kiva mural with a contemporaneous Mexica codex depiction of Tlazolteotl illustrates Chalchihuitlicue in a startlingly similar manner (Figure 37). This same artistic movement introduces bands of water, populated with various water creatures (Smith 1952: Plate D). Whatever this phenomenon was which took root in the Hopi pueblos, it missed the Upland Salado completely. The only Upland Salado room which I know of as having special wall treatment was the late kiva-like ceremonial room at Besh-Ba-Gowah, which was plastered with creamy white clay, not painted. Pigments were available locally in red, yellow, black, blue, green, and white, but were only used on baskets, arrow shafts, long wands, gaming sticks, and shields, not walls.

One potter at Besh-Ba-Gowah made small, hemispherical, incurving, early Gila Polychrome bowls with water creatures in the bottom surrounded by double cloud terraces. She may also have made the katsina mask bowl with the rainbow motif curving over the face (Figure 27). Another prolific potter, or potter family, at Besh-Ba-Gowah made bowls in Gila Polychrome and Cliff Polychrome decorated with bands of diagonal parallel lines alternating with descending water squiggles which are found in many local sites, even as far away as Tonto Cliff Dwellings. Water motifs, water creature motifs, horned/feathered serpent motifs, medicinal plants, and Morning and Evening Star Crosses are favorite subjects of pottery decoration.

In the north, rock art was an adjunct to the Katsina Cult. Locally, the only rock art is in the upper Dripping Springs drainage. It is in the form of petroglyphs. Its time span appears to extend from Archaic to Yavapai and Apache (Figures 38 and 39).

The influence of Kayenta immigrants at Besh-Ba-Gowah seems to have impacted Gila Pueblo until the ca. A.D. 1385 renovation. Then, the attention of these local Salados seems to have turned to the south and east. Cliff Polychrome becomes fashionable for cooking ware. The *piki* stone is broken and its hearth is remodeled to accommodate a Cliff Polychrome cooking bowl. Cobbled areas are installed as bases for large granary baskets, suggesting a change in feasting custom. The ceremonial focus at Gila Pueblo goes from centralized to dispersed. At first, ceremonial objects are few in number and concentrated in Room 110, and its backstage Room 105. Then, after the renovation of the pueblo, ceremonial objects become more numerous and more scattered throughout the households, as if each lineage were responsible for the care of its ceremonial equipment. This period appears to involve a variety of approaches to the unseen universe which includes shamanism, curanderismo, the use of the water drum, and avoidance of menstruating women. Amadeo Rea presents a helpful summary of the activities of Piman shamans and healers, which may reflect the belief system prevalent in the late Prehispanic period (Rea 2007a: 45-51).

The most frequent question I have been asked since the publication of *Southwest Birds of Sacrifice* is "What comprised the belief system present in the Southwest before the introduction of the Mesoamerican god cults?" Most basic is the concept of complementary duality, the shaman and the midwife, brought from the old world. There is also ample evidence of the importance of the sun, moon, circumpolar constellations which are always visible, and of Venus as the Morning Star and Evening Star. Another basic concept is the Flower World.

The Salado Shaman and the Rattlesnake Curandera

Conventional archaeological thought has been willing to consider shamanic activity among early and mobile populations in the Southwest, but it has tended to concentrate on "organized religion" in pueblo societies. Nevertheless, indications of shamanic practice continue to appear in Mimbres pictorial pottery (Figures 12 and 39), and in the presence of quartz crystal fragments on the ground floor of Room 101 at Gila Pueblo.

Gila Pueblo Room 101 contained a large number of quartz crystal fragments, in addition to a selenite crystal 40 cm in length. Room 101 was also the entry to the secluded back stage Room 105, which lay behind the slat altar, and from behind which dramatic presentations could be staged for the benefit of the audience in Room 110. The process of getting into Room 105 involved going down two ladders and through a door at the bottom, much like entering a cave. The cave motif is a common shamanic visualization. Room 101 is an ideal location for a shamanic practitioner (Figure 38).

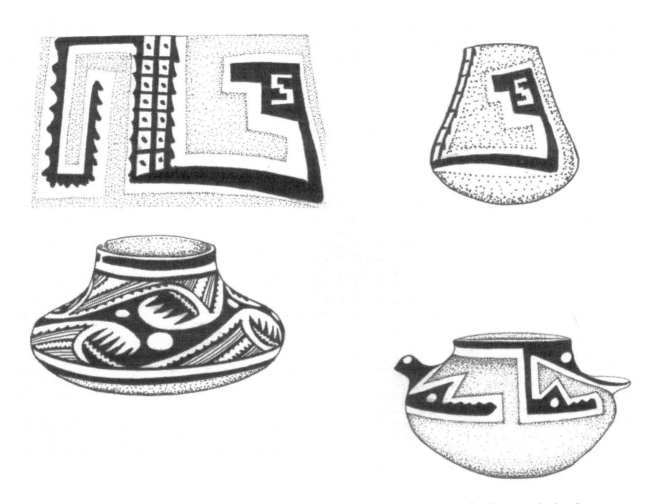

Figure 36. Tonto Polychrome: Serpent and Tlaloc Eye Motifs. <u>Top</u>: serpent of unknown derivation. <u>Bottom-left</u>: running feathered serpent with Tlaloc eyes in negative, derived from water dog. <u>Bottom-right</u>: quail effigy decorated with stylized horn worms with Tlaloc eyespots in negative. All from Besh-Ba-Gowah.

In my experience, the success of shamanic practice is transactional. The client must be willing to accept the good offices of the practitioner. They must be thankful for the help. They must show the practitioner <u>respect</u>. Then, when they thank him or her wholeheartedly, and give the practitioner an appropriate token of appreciation, their subconscious will recognize that work has been done, and it is okay to accept a new operational program and begin to heal.

Shamanic practice within the Casas Grandes Trading Network was facilitated by assistants, shaman's stools, prayer sticks, and feather containers including rolls of matting, long baskets, or boxes with handles. The shaman illustrated in Figure 38 sits upon a shaman's stool and holds a feather container. His assistant holds a prayer stick. The assistant is essential to his practice because it is the assistant's duty to protect his body while he is absent in shamanic

Figure 37. Copulating Couple and Woman-of-Power Motifs. <u>Top-left</u>: Mimbres B/w bowl design, after Moulard 1981: Plate 9. <u>Top-center</u>: similar Dripping Springs petroglyph, after Kelly Byrne photo. <u>Top-right</u>: dissimilar stylized, Santa Cruz R/buff bowl design, after Moulard 1981: Plate 57. <u>Middle</u>: Awatovi kiva mural, Room 529. Inverted Black God with Pleiades on mask; left, Chalchihuitlicue offers herself to Ce Ácatl; center, Ce Ácatl casts a dart at Chalchihuitlicue's leg; right, the dart passes through (impregnates) her womb; birth canal is visible below. After Smith 1952: Figure 53. <u>Bottom</u>: Chalchihuitlicue similar to above; Tlazolteotl/Spider Grandmother holds serpent of wisdom and spindle indicative of her power as an Elder Woman and restorer, simplified from Gonzales 2012: 91.

trance, and to "talk him home" should he fail to return to his body at the expected time. The shaman illustrated in Figure 11 holds a rattle, and has a long, flat feather box with a handle. This box could also contain bone sucking tubes, mineral concretions, fossils, animal bones, herbs, fetishes, or other items necessary to his practice. His left foot is on backwards, indicating his association with, Xolotl, "Younger Brother," the patron of shamans. Stools of the type shown in Figure 38 survive, rendered in stone, at Paquimé (DiPeso 1974: Volume 2, pp. 577, 580, Figure 367-2).

Figure 38. Shaman, Assistant, and Deer Dancers. <u>Left</u>: shaman sits on shaman's stool holding feather container; assistant holds prayer stick, Mimbres B/w bowl design, after Brody and others 1983: 99. <u>Center</u>: deer dancer petroglyph from Dripping Springs, after Kelly Byrne photo. <u>Right</u>: two views of argillite bead in the form of a deer dancer, local but unprovenienced. Scale: x 1.

The content of the medicine pouches of the two Gila Pueblo men wearing "Summer People" Moiety leadership costumes included mineral concretions, an obsidian nodule, quartz crystal, corn kernels, a copper bell, a flake scraper, and an antique Clovis point. Although these persons appeared to be more involved in secular than in sacred leadership at the time of their death, it is obvious from their shaman-like possessions that there was a mixture of responsibility. Social, religious, and political functions were probably not separable in their community.

The midwife of ancient times, with her string apron, is the prototype, first, for Raven's Wife; and, later, for Chalchihuitlicue, Our Lady Precious Green; for the Green Woman of the peyote quest, and probably also for the Zuni Rattlesnake Priestess and her local version at Besh-Ba-Gowah (see the section on Datura in this work). *Curanderismo* is still practiced in the Southwest and Northwestern Mexico in an aboriginal-derived form (Gonzales 2012). The practice is covered in detail by Gonzales, an expert on and practitioner of *Curanderismo* in her book, *Red Medicine*. It's probably as close as we are going to get to an understanding of pre-contact women's spirituality. Gonzales discusses Spider Grandmother, the ultimate woman of power. At Gila Pueblo and Besh-Ba-Gowah, the women of power appear as the high-status burial of a maiden, the matron with the crimson skirt and shell stomacher, and the crone with her broken hip, who was spinning under the ramada on top of the ceremonial/redistribution complex when Gila Pueblo fell. Spider Grandmother is there as the crone, but the Woman of Power is also expressed as the maid and matron, following the lunar phases. The fourth phase, the dark of the moon, is present as the ancestral women interred in the family's favored place of burial, and living their lives in the land of the departed.

The Flower World

Throughout the Uto-Aztecan speaking Southwest and Mesoamerica, there is a continuum of a beneficent, beautiful, shining, flowery world, which exists in time from the Archaic to the present. The Flower World is strongly associated with the singing of beautiful poetry, but may also be illustrated in pottery design (Figure 27, lower-left). It is easy to see, in this arid region, that infrequent wet years would produce such an awe-inspiring event that it would remain in memory, and be perpetuated in tradition. My husband, Robert, saw the desert bloom once in a rainy year in the 1940s, and then not again until the spring of 1969. That year, the flowers were so spectacular we drove all the way from Globe to San Carlos and back, astonished at the desert hills suddenly covered with magenta owl clover, which we had never seen before, as well as a multitude of other flowers, the seeds of which had lain dormant for decades (compare to Huckell and VanPool 2006: 156)

Among the Aztecs, the Flower World appears as Tlalocan, the place of Tlaloc and Chalchihuitlicue, a watery, verdant land of perpetual spring, abounding in corn, amaranth, squash, beans, chilies, tomatoes, and marigolds (Miller and Taube 1993: 167).

The Huichol Peyote Quest takes place as a guided meditation which places the participants in the Flower World. The participants encounter the Green Woman, a present-day manifestation of Chalchihuitlicue, patron of water on the surface of the earth, the little pools of water which are dripped into gourds with an arrow shaft, a fertility custom, and the peyote gathering which is enacted as a deer hunt. In the deer-hunt enactment, the first peyote found is shot with an arrow. The entire expedition is staged as a ceremonial deer hunt, which is a device for renewal. Corn, deer, and peyote are a traditional unit in the sustenance of the people.

Moving northward, the Pimas have, or at least had, a guided healing meditation involving the Flower World, which I was taught in the summer of 1970 by Ammie Ray Elkins, an Anglo *Curandero* who practiced in Globe from 1970 until the late 1980s. Ray, the son of a Southern Pacific Railroad employee, grew up on the Pima Reservation in the 1930s, was a fluent speaker of the Pima language, and received the ceremonial education, instruction in herbology, and initiations of a Pima boy of the time. In this meditation, the participant climbed up a path over a little desert hill, to where one could walk down into a green valley. The deer browsed and the rabbits nibbled peacefully. A shallow stream could be heard as it flowed. Fragrant flowers bloomed, birds sang; and insects buzzed. The sun was warm, the shade was cool, and one could lie down on the soft grass to rest and heal. It was possible to leave this valley or return to it as needed.

The Hopi and their neighbors regard the Flower World with its moisture, water creatures, dragonflies, fluttering butterflies, singing birds, and blossoming plants not as a remote heaven, but as achievable in this world. To quote Hayes-Gilpin, Newsome, and Sekaquaptewa (2010: p. 137), "In this world, hardship, contradiction, conflict, death, and sacrifice are all as necessary and natural as the good things that hard work, prayer, song, and humility ultimately bring about."

Hayes-Gilpin, Newsome, and Sekaquaptewa (2010: 122-123) describe the Flower World as existing from ancient times in song, and then assuming material form in some kiva murals, and in Sikyatki Polychrome pottery designs.

The Hopi Way is a tiny island of austerity set in an enormous and magnificent landscape. One is not Hopi by ethnicity; one chooses to live this life of hard work where ritual observance is as important as toiling in the corn field. Depictions in kiva murals of elements of the Flower World appear to involve sodalities, rather than the whole population (Hays-Gilpin 2006: 68-78). Given that kiva murals are the work of sodalities, their spread was facilitated, and they traveled to and fro across the northern agglomerated pueblos, as did the mixtures of styles. This late flurry of artistic expression crosscut linguistic barriers and also the barriers of the old Casas Grandes and Hohokam shell trade networks. It does not appear to have had any effect upon the Upland Salados.

Pertinent to the Upland Salados would have been the Flower World, which survives in southern Arizona, conveyed in the beautiful songs that accompany the Yaqui Deer Dance. Yaqui cosmology has a number of realms that can be experienced through dream or trance. The experience one has in these realms may be transmitted by sung deer dance poetry. The *yo ania* is a realm of power. White-tailed deer may emerge from it and confer power on an individual (Evers and Molina 1987:45-46). The *sea ania* is the Flower World, a wilderness in the sense of wild-deer-ness, covered with flowers. The deer songs were first used to placate the White-tailed deer, and render him willing to be killed. All Yaqui deer songs describe the Flower World (Evers and Molina 1987: 51).

During our trip to Mexico in March of 2011, Robert and I had the opportunity one evening in El Fuerte, Sinaloa, to witness a deer dance performed by Mayo Indians who were part of the University of Sinaloa traditional dance group. As the participants prepared for their performance, one young Mayo staggered out, struggling to carry a large, oval, antique, gray enamelware baby bath, partially filled with water, without spilling it. He then added two large pitchers of water, to raise the level to the desired depth. The oval baby bath was just large enough to accommodate the large, bi-lobed bottle gourd with its bulbous neck and base. The side of the lower, larger chamber had been cut out, and the orifice was submerged. He held the neck with his left hand, and drummed on the larger, lower portion with a padded stick held in his right hand.

As dusk fell, the deer dancer appeared, his antlers bedecked with red strips of cloth, large gourd rattles in his hands, his kilt overlain by deer-hoof tinklers around his hips, and his lower legs wrapped in bands of rattles made of the cocoons of giant silk moths, Family *Saturniidae,* (Peigler 1994). He came forth tentatively, like a fawn, grew in power, fled from the hunters, became exhausted, was killed, and then rose again in renewal, and returned to the Flower World.

Many unanswered questions remained from the late twentieth century excavations at Besh-Ba-Gowah, Pinal Pueblo, Hagen Site, and Gila Pueblo. One was the use of large, oval-shaped, gaudily decorated Tonto Polychrome bowls, about 45 cm long and 25 cm wide, recovered from the high-status male burial at Pinal Pueblo, and from Room 98 at Gila Pueblo.

Another was the use of an antlered deer cranium which appeared to have been hung from the rafters of the second story of Room 110, a possible Hunting Society room. In the site report, my students and I speculated that it might have something to do with hide dressing, but we were not at all happy with this interpretation. Hide dressing is a nasty, messy, smelly operation, and we didn't really think it appropriate for a society room in a ceremonial complex. Then, a third problem arose when the kind offices of Philip DeMario of Globe transferred to us a donated bead. It was made from local argillite and depicted a deer dancer, (Figure 38).

Deer dancer headdresses have changed even in historic times. Photographs from the 1930s show one as a skull, jaws, and neck vertebrae, covered with dried skin. A deer dance head dress we observed at Pascua Village, Tucson, Arizona, on Good Friday, 1952, consisted of the antlered cranium, worn like a cap and secured under the chin with thongs. The horns were bedecked with red satin ribbons. There were no lower jaws. The skin was sewn together under the palate. The antlered cranium which hung in the rafters of Room 110 may have been a headdress of this type.

During the excavation at Gila Pueblo, my students and I looked in vain for deer scapula rasps, for deer scapulae with perforated articulations which could be used as clappers, and for bird-bone flutes. We did find turtle shell, which could have come from a rattle, but deer dancers today use gourd rattles. Deer dancers are accompanied by singers of beautiful poetry; and by musicians playing the water drum with a stick padded with corn husks, and playing wooden rasps placed on a half gourd and sounded with a slender rod (Evers and Molina 1987: 6, 34, 41, 52, 68, 70 82, 87). Deer dance occasions also involve music played by a *tampaleo,* a musician who plays a five-tone flute and a shallow two-headed drum simultaneously, and by violin and harp (Evers and Molina 1987: 16, 81). All of these instruments, as well as the rattles carried, the deer hoof tinklers, and the giant silk moth cocoon *tenevoim* worn by the deer dancer, are biodegradable, except for the water drum bowl. We did find oval pottery bowls, which may be water drums. At this point, in light of the deer dancer bead, I believe that the antlered deer cranium we found is better interpreted as evidence of deer dancing at Gila Pueblo, rather than hide dressing. Two presumed Tonto Polychrome water drum bowls were found, one with a warrior burial at Pinal Pueblo, and one in what appears to be a women's society room at Gila Pueblo. Water drums are used for both deer dancing and childbirth ceremonies (Gonzales 2010:238).

Danny (Daniel) Leon, a Yaqui from Old Pascua, has painted at least two murals depicting a deer dancer in the Flower World, one at Old Pascua in Tucson in August of 1980 (pictured and discussed in Evers and Molina 1987: frontispiece, 59-61), and another at the Arizona State Museum in 1993 (Sheridan and Parezo 1996: Plate 6). Although deer dancing is generally thought of as a Yaqui phenomenon, it is also present among the Mayo and Mountain Tarahumara. Amadeo Rea reports that Yaqui deer dancers not only perform for Pimas and Tohono O'odham, but may also teach them to dance (personal communication, January 2013).

Looking Toward the South: Women's Spirituality

Clara Lee Tanner had a custom of putting subjects she didn't want to answer questions about in the last sentence of her lectures. The use of psychoactive substances was one such subject and women's spirituality was another. I have been attempting to reconstruct prehistoric women's spirituality for over 60 years. Until recently, most archaeologists were men, and the Native Americans with whom they conversed were men. All of them answered my questions in the same way, "We don't know. Women's spirituality is too sacred to talk about." That is what they said. What they really meant, whether they knew it or not, is that the doings of women of child-bearing age are too *dangerous*, too *powerful*, to talk about. European contact has deprived us of the heritage of many southern Arizona groups.

Ruth Underhill (1965: 57), however, presents a consideration of the Tohono O'odham which is helpful. She saw them as living dual lives. During the growing season they lived agricultural lives, and participated in agricultural ceremonies conducted by priestly officiants. During the remainder of the year they turned to hunting and gathering, and respected the medicine man, the vision, woman power, and dread of the dead. Except for fear of the dead, their religious expressions accord well with the practices which appear to have been carried out late in the occupation of Gila Pueblo.

At about the summer solstice, when the saguaro fruit ripens, the first raindrops of the pre-monsoon fall and the wandering Tohono-O'odham return to their homes, a saguaro-wine ceremony is held for fertility. It involves circle dancing, smoking, singing beautiful poetry, drinking, and vomiting. Vomiting is considered especially efficacious in bringing rain throughout the Southwest and Mesoamerica. Although there are no saguaros at the altitude of the Salado pueblos, there is abundant agave and cactus fruit which could have been used in brewing. The Tarahumara make beer out of dried corn by soaking it, sprouting it in baskets, grinding the sprouted corn on a metate, and then liquefying it with water. Various herbs are added to help it ferment, and otherwise fortify it. The resulting beer is low in alcohol, but high in calories. It must be consumed quickly, before it turns to vinegar (Richard Fisher, personal communication, November 2010).

Another custom of the Tohono-O'odham, which may have some significance in relationship to Gila Pueblo, is the seclusion of menstruating women. Women must hide themselves at this time so that they are not even looked upon by hunters, for fear that the hunters may become unsuccessful, perhaps even unsuccessful for life. This of course goes back to the ancient concept of Raven as the patron of hunters, and Raven's Wife as patron of game animals. Raven's Wife gave the game animals the sense of smell so they could escape the hunters, maintaining a balance between the hunter and the hunted (Luckert 1976: p. 36). A small structure south of Gila Pueblo, labeled "Field House" in the lower-right of Figure 28, may actually have served as a place of concealment for menstruating women. The crimson apron worn by the high-status lady found formally laid out with her children in Room 110, may also signify this frighteningly powerful period in women's lives.

Room 98, Gila Pueblo, may be a woman's society meeting room. Its most conspicuous feature was a bowling-ball-sized greenstone sphere. Frank and Carol Crosswhite, formerly of the Boyce Thompson Arboretum in Superior, told me the O'odham ceremonialists at Quitobac displayed a sacred basket containing a green stone, half of the Earth Monster's heart, at a ceremony which re-enacted the creation of the world. It appears that this is the same baseball-sized greenstone, kept nested on eagle feathers in a deer skin bag, lashed in a basket, which was reported by Davis (1920: 162-164). The Room 98 greenstone sphere may be a similar representation. It may have been hidden from the view of profane eyes in a bundle or basket. Mesoamericans associate green stone with Chalchihuitlicue, Our Lady Precious Green, who was the patron of springs, pools, and streams which occurred naturally on the surface of the earth, as well as the watery womb, birth, and baptism (Miller and Taube 1993: 60).

The storage pit in Room 98 contained the neck bones of a female Small Indian Domestic Turkey, which was a trade specialty of the Tompiro Pueblos in central New Mexico. This phenotype is small, short legged, hump-backed, dark colored, and has a neck feathered all the way to the head (McKusick 1986: 26). It occurs after 300 B.C. in the Southwest as a sacrifice to Tlaloc, patron of rain and underground water (McKusick 2001:42-49). My daughters heard me mumbling to myself about, "Why would anyone make a fetish out of a turkey neck?" They dissolved in gales of laughter, exclaiming in unison, "Because it looks like an umbilical cord!" They are right; it does.

A third unusual artifact from Room 98 is the large oval Tonto Polychrome bowl placed against the east wall, which may be a water drum. Water drums are used to accompany deer dancers, but they are also used during traditional childbirth ceremonies (Gonzales 2012: 237-238).

Female Moon and Venus Phases

Human gestation marks a coincidence of the Lunar and Venus Cycles. Mesoamericans count gestation as 20×13 days, or a 260-day Venus Cycle roughly equivalent to 9×29 days, or a 261-day, nine-month Lunar Cycle. The imagery of the woman as maid, matron, crone, and woman in the underworld is present in Mesoamerican art (Figure 6). However, in Mimbres art the maid is seldom pictured, and the matron appears most often as Mother Earth, bearing the Venus Twins or the Sun Antelope across the sky on her basket (Figures 15 and 40). The only Mimbres representation of a mortal woman of power I can identify is the lady pictured in Figure 29. She wears a costume identical to that of the Red Apron Lady laid out as an altar piece during the closing activities in Room 110. Spindles, which signify a crone/female elder in Mesoamerican art, are reminiscent of the spindle whorl found next to the body of the old crippled woman killed on the second-story roof of Room 110. Gonzales (2012: 91, 95) pictures the powerful woman as Tlazolteotl, the defender and begetter, patron of time, medicine, weaving, and Mexica merchants (Figure 37). Tlazolteotl holds both spindles and the serpent of wisdom. She is often pictured in conjunction with a centipede and a serpent, entwined to form the sign for "movement." With her are the recumbent Chalchihuitlicue, and the Ehecatl "Breath of Life" manifestation of Venus, instead of the more common Ce Ácatl manifestation of Venus as the Morning Star Warrior, a reference to impregnation (compare Smith 1952, Figure 53; Brundage 1979:109: and Burland and Forman 1975: 45).

A lot of women's spirituality is subliminal, rather than obvious. For example, if I go to gather herbs, they are often in my garden or close at hand, and can be picked on the way home from doing something else. I can pick herbs and nobody notices. On the other hand, if my husband went to gather herbs, it involved an expedition, either to a higher altitude to pick Yerbasanta, *Eriodictyon* sp., or to Dripping Springs to pick Creosote Bush, *Larrea tridentata*. He had to make preparations; he has to take someone with him; and he had to let us know when to expect him back. When he picked herbs, in comparison, it was a big deal.

Sun Transit Motifs

Sun mask motifs are not apparent in Mimbres and Salado art. The sun is symbolized in Mimbres art by deer, antelope, and quail (Brundage 1979:38). Quail painted on Mimbres bowls mark the sun transit, bearing the Morning Star motif for sunrise, the Mountain Evening Primrose flower for sunset, and the Milky Way polka dot pattern for night (Figure 39). Deer and antelope are not apparent in Salado art, but the quail appears in effigy jar form in Gila Polychrome ca. A.D. 1340, and in Tonto Polychrome in the 1440s. At Besh-Ba-Gowah, polychrome bird effigies were more often associated with female burials. At Gila Pueblo, they were associated with other ceremonial artifacts which appeared to be in male usage.

Center Places

The concept of a center place is expressed in many ways in the pre-Hispanic Southwest. The archaeological pueblo site of Casa Malpais, near Springerville, Arizona, may be the model for a three-level framework of the visible universe. At this site one can see the remains of a great kiva, a kiva, and on a lower level, a woman's society room. Outside the entrance of the great kiva is a stone plug which may be lifted to view the roof and hatch of an underground kiva built within a volcanic tube. These volcanic tubes were used as burial caves, and are still receiving offerings by pueblo peoples. According to the archaeologists who dug the site, they may not be entered. Breaking this restriction, they say, has resulted in inescapable fatal supernatural sanctions. However, just knowing the burial chambers are there is sufficient. The sky arches overhead, mankind lives on the surface of the earth, and the departed take up their existence in a visible underworld.

Gila Pueblo has a parallel construction. Room 110 has a second-story roof with a ramada on top, a second-story society room in the middle, and a ground-floor ceremonial room with a slat altar on the bottom floor. There was a raised area for a fire to illuminate the slat altar, and a foot-square hole in the room floor above. The hole was probably provided with a cover which may have been closed most of the time. However, it is easy to visualize it being opened so that small children could view a dramatic presentation of mythological subjects enacted in the "underworld" below.

At Besh-Ba-Gowah, families used the same burial places over and over. Patio 77 is an example. The patio is large enough to bury a large number of people singly, but the preference was to use the same hole, disturbing the bones of previous burials. Two factors appear to influence this choice. First, the departed were transferred directly into their family's underworld household. Secondly, there is a strong belief among Uto-Aztecan speakers that bones in the ground are very important. There is a Mesoamerican myth in which the posthumous son of the previous day's sun stops to hunt quail, at which moment the bones of the old sun turn into a deer which springs away to the north, streaming rays of light (Brundage 1979:38). Bones in the

Figure 39. Moon, Venus, and Sun Transit Motifs. <u>Top Row, Maya glyphs:</u> left: moon; center: Venus as morning and evening star; right: sun, after Coe 2011: 235. <u>Second Row, Mimbres B/w:</u> left: quail with Milky Way design, sun in the underworld, Cameron Creek Village, after Bradfield 1931: Plate LXXVI; left center: quail with Mountain Evening Primrose sunset design; right center: quail with Venus as morning star sunrise design, after Cosgrove and Cosgrove 1932: Plate 215; far right: Sunflower sun in daytime design, after Bradfield, 1929: Plate LIV. <u>Third Row, Mimbres B/w:</u> left: Mother Earth carries Venus as Morning and Evening Star across the sky on her basket, after Davis 1995: 155; right: similar transit bearing the sun antelope, sun in daytime design, after Davis 1995:157. <u>Fourth Row, Mimbres B/w:</u> left: moon woman garbed as moon rabbit, depicting lunar transit, after Brody and others 1983: 68; right: woman, boy and dog gathering wood, depicting sun near the winter solstice and son/posthumous son of the sun mythology, Mimbres B/w, Cienega Site, after Brody and others 1983: 93.

ground are like seeds in the ground. Once they are planted, they are expected to come forth again. There is a recurring theme of renewal, rebirth, "climb the ladder," and "you've got to do it right this time."

In the household, the center place was the hearth. In a woman, the center place was her womb. In a man, the center place may have been the burial place of his umbilical stump. For the woman's society at Gila Pueblo, it may have been the green stone sphere, or the turkey neck concealed in the storage pit in the floor of Room 98. If Grasshopper, Besh-Ba-Gowah, and Gila Pueblo are viewed as feminine icons, then the covered entry passages are birth canals, and the paired patios represent wombs.

In summary, it appears that in the A.D. 1440s, Salado religious outlook preserved the shaman and assistant, the midwife, and the rattlesnake *curandera* on one hand, had adopted the Flower World, Deer Dancer complex, and Poorwill creation myth (Rea 2007b), from the desert tribes to the south on the other, and still maintained a semi-priestly socio/politico/religious organization in the middle which coordinated recurring yearly observances

9—The End of the Upland Salado Occupation

Pueblo IV Population Clusters

Maps of Pueblo IV settlements in the Southwest generally indicate large pueblos of 1000 rooms or more. Small settlements of only 200+ rooms, like Besh-Ba-Gowah and Gila Pueblo, though they may be vigorous production and trading centers, are seldom included. The conditions under which populations in this area lived in the A.D. 1440s are best considered relative to their inclusion in a population center. Wilcox, Robertson, and Wood (2001: Figure 7.15, 166), picture the Besh-Ba-Gowah population cluster as having 166 – 350 rooms. This is unrealistic. Besh-Ba-Gowah and Gila Pueblo both had more than 200 rooms. Besh-Ba-Gowah had a rectangular outlier just uphill from the main roomblock, as well as the ca. 35-room Pinal Pueblo across Sixshooter Canyon. Gila Pueblo had an approximately 40 room outlier, the Derringer Drive Site just across the wash to its west, as well as the 17 rooms of the Hagen Site to its south. Then there are the nearby Bar-F-Bar and Gap sites, and a very large pueblo at the junction of Russel Gulch and Pinal Creek which now lies under the Cobre Valley Shopping Center. Between the Pinal Creek drainage and San Carlos are three more sites, Cutter, Ranch Creek, and Gilson Ranch. All these sites are Gila Phase, and aggregate far more than 1000+ rooms in their population cluster, but they are still separate entities, and are therefore not noted on maps. The important consideration at this time period is that population clusters were separated by expanses of no man's land.

We know from the trade items and common iconography present at the fall of Gila Pueblo which surviving population centers were of importance to local commerce. Zuni to the northeast was connected to Gila Pueblo by Salado polychrome pottery, by datura and Hawk Moth iconography on local polychrome pottery, by owl and other pottery bird effigies, by beads and fetishes carved in imitation of life forms, and by the probability of Zuni-type rattlesnake *curanderas,* among women buried at Besh-Ba-Gowah. Zuni is a probable market for the large quantity of cotton, and/or cotton cloth production of Gila Pueblo. Gila Pueblo was connected to Gran Quivira on the east, as exemplified by the presence of bones of a Small Indian Domestic phenotype turkey, which was a trade specialty of the Tompiro Pueblos; and by an imported Chupadero Black-on-white pitcher (Figure 35, Room 102, upper-right). Gila Pueblo was connected to Paquimé to the southeast by imports of macaws, copper bells, and trumpets made from *Strombus, Hexaplex, Murex,* and *Melongena* shells. In exchange, they could have offered polychrome pottery, ground pigments, and Sleeping Beauty Turquoise (Vokes and Gregory 2007: 326-327, 333-334. 339-340, 342).

Dripping Springs Valley, 16 miles by jeep road over the Pinal Mountains through the pass between Signal Peak on the east and Madera Peak on the west, lies within the Besh-Ba-Gowah population cluster boundary. It shares the adobe bottom step of the ladder trait with Gila Pueblo (Smith 1979: 47-48). Philip Smith, who excavated a number of partially vandalized sites in the area, noted only seven Tonto Polychrome vessels, in only one of his three sites (Smith 1979: 52). Examination of his illustrations revealed only two Cliff Polychrome bowls (Smith 1979: 69, bottom and right center). Thus, it appears that the Dripping Springs Valley was abandoned before either Tonto Polychrome or Cliff Polychrome became really popular, and that refugees fleeing the destruction of Gila Pueblo would not have found shelter that close.

All the late pueblos in the Globe-Miami area were destroyed with significant loss of life, and burned. Gila Pueblo has evidence of the incorporation of residents of, first, Pinal Pueblo, and second, Besh-Ba-Gowah. This is based on designs painted on pottery recovered from the latest-built rooms at Gila Pueblo, which were characteristic of those found at Pinal Pueblo and at Besh-Ba-Gowah. Apparently, as pueblos fell, survivors found protection with neighboring pueblos where they had kinsmen or clansmen. Some survivors may have traveled even farther. When the last pueblo fell, the only place left to flee was to a settlement where one had trading partners. In the case of Gila Pueblo, they may have sought refuge with the Zuni to the north, or perhaps the desert tribes to the south. The possibility of deer dancing, and of the seclusion of menstruation women, makes the southern choice more probable. Then, there is the matter of distance and language. The Upland Salados are in a Uto-Aztecan language area. The tribes to the south were closer, and spoke Uto-Aztecan. Zuni was much farther away and its inhabitants spoke a different language (Gregory and Wilcox 20008: 19).

The Destruction of Gila Pueblo

When Gila Pueblo was attacked and its population decimated in the A.D. 1440s, the bodies left lying dead where they had fallen were of four types: the very old, the very young, the pregnant women, and the leadership. Not counting the dead from Room 111, because of extensive disturbance by an apparent Yavapai reoccupation, the bodies of seventy persons slain in the attack were unearthed during the Eastern Arizona College excavation. There were two in utero; 12 infants, 0-2 years; 14 small children, 2-7 years; 3 large children, 8-10 years; one adolescent 11-21 years; 3 young adults, 21-25 years; 28 adults, 26-39 years; and 8 old adults, 40+ years (McKusick and Young 1997: 111-114). The pregnant women were one young adult, 21-25 years, and one adult 26-39 years. Fourteen of these lay slain within Room 105, or at its door, the most inaccessible area of the ceremonial/redistribution complex, where they had apparently hoped to hide.

The dearth of most of the large children, adolescents, and young adults, led us to believe that the motive for the A.D. 1440s raid on Gila Pueblo was the same as the apparent motive of the 1260 raid: slaves. The projectile points used in both instances were the same: thin, well-flaked triangular points without side or basal notching (Figure 30). William Underwood, who excavated along the Salt River, recognized these as characteristic of points produced at the Armer Ranch Site, which is located on the margin of the Cline Terrace population center nearest to the Besh-Ba-Gowah population center. When we were preparing the manuscript for *The Gila Pueblo Salado,* Jon Young and I were unaware that Rice and Redman had published an article in *Native Peoples Magazine,* which stated that Cline Terrace platform mound was active until shortly after A.D. 1450 (Rice and Redman 1992: 24). This extended life span for the Cline Terrace community provides a logical motive for the A.D. 1440s raid on Gila Pueblo.

The Use of Alcohol and Herbal Doping Agents

When the manuscript for the Casas Grandes report was in preparation, I suggested to Charles Di Peso that the raid which destroyed Paquimé came at about the time of the Spring Equinox, based upon the age at death of the macaws which had perished in that disaster. He responded with the information that the mescal pits were full at the time of the raid, confirming the Spring Equinox date. The consumption of alcoholic beverages at religious festivals, or to provide easily assimilated calories for the purpose of accomplishing projects requiring hard physical labor, whether in southern Arizona or among the Tarahumara in northern Mexico, continues today. In addition, the beverages may be fortified with herbal concoctions to increase endurance. Clara Lee Tanner emphasized the need to administer emetics and cathartics to the participants in katsina dances and other dances after they were held in the Hopi pueblos. At the time of this lecture, I assumed that it was a ritual cleansing, but later, when I attended a Butterfly Dance, I realized it was also a physical cleansing. The tiny old men who drummed and chanted to accompany the dancers performed vigorously throughout a set, and then disappeared into a house on the plaza to, as Clara Lee Tanner put it, "refresh themselves." Shortly, they returned, reinvigorated, and began to drum again. At the time I could not understand how such old people could be so vigorous, and drum for set after set of dancing, throughout an entire afternoon. Now, after having talked to Tarahumara *curandera,* Sra. Conchita Mancinas, I have come to realize that herbal doping agents were, and are still, in common usage.

Clara Lee Tanner gave a lecture in another class about Tarahumara foot racing. The Tarahumara of the Sierra Madre Occidental are noted for their speed and endurance. The women race with a small cloth-wrapped circlet which they pick up with a stick and throw ahead of them. This race has fertility significance, and is apparently of long standing. It sounds like a slow process, but the race is amazingly swift. A similar circlet, in Mimbres art, appears in Figure 29. Men race with a wooden ball, which they scoop up with their sandaled foot and cast ahead of them. They carry a lath-like fetching stick to extract the ball from brush or cactus if it should go astray from the desired course. The men's race appears to be a simile for the passage of the sun across the sky. Clara Lee Tanner also related the tradition of the relentless Tarahumara hunter running a deer until it fell dead of exhaustion. I now realize that these runners use "false peyote" as a doping agent to enable them to accomplish this feat.

Given that the fall of Paquimé coincided with the Spring Equinox, and the fall of Gila Pueblo coincided with the Fall Equinox, as indicated by crops drying upon the rooftops, it is reasonable to suppose that the attackers took advantage of an occasion when the inhabitants might be found in some state of ritual inebriation, to conduct their raid with less opposition.

Trade as a Means of Entry into a Pueblo

Attendance at a religious observance was, and is, often accompanied by a market day. On Gila Pueblo's final day, nests of three polychrome bowls, and cooking jars were set out on the rooftop, as if offered for trade. The raiders could have walked in as visitors to the pueblo on a festive occasion and then, when they were in a position to strike down the leadership, they could have launched a surprise attack. In any case, there was little if any attempt at resistance on the part of the inhabitants apart from attempting to hide.

Vulture and Raven Migration Patterns

Some turkey vultures and common ravens live and nest in the canyons and in the large trees downstream from Besh-Ba-Gowah. However, in September of each year, large numbers of vultures and additional ravens gather in these trees on their yearly migration. Their numbers are greatest at the time of the Fall Equinox; then they sail south into Mexico on the last of the summer thermals. They are not seen again until the Spring Equinox, when they sail north on the thermals to their summer feeding grounds. Vultures are large heavy birds which rely on a finite supply of carrion for their food. They cannot afford to flap to fly; they must sail to travel efficiently. The bodies lying on the roof tops at Gila Pueblo were not disarrayed; but they were quickly de-fleshed, as confirmed by physical anthropologists at the Arizona State Museum. Their hair pins remained firmly attached, and their bones were articulated when the pueblo burned. Vultures are dainty and efficient eaters. Migrating vultures could have swooped in, wave after wave, and left the bodies as we found them, articulated but burned in a de-fleshed state.

Site-closing Activities

When we excavated Gila Pueblo, everything was as it had been left on that final day with a few exceptions. A large flaring feasting bowl decorated with swirling Poorwill designs, and splattered with carbonized gruel, was smashed and scattered across the roof tops. This bowl was enormous, in excess of 40 cm in diameter, and was similar in shape to one recovered from the NAN Ranch Site in the Mimbres Valley of New Mexico (Shafer 2003: 241, Figure A.8 D–F). In ceremonial Room 110, the body of a mature, high-status woman wearing a crimson cochineal-dyed string apron and a 6000–7000 shell-bead stomacher caught up at the sides with what appeared to be whale ear bones, was laid out with her two children, just as if she was in a grave or was an altar piece. A Tonto Polychrome beaker, decorated with centipedes and water zigzags, stood nearby.

Three bodies of adult males, who we assumed were killed on the first-story roof, were found stacked one atop the other, tee-pee fashion, on the floor of Room 102. They were symmetrically placed, resting on their foreheads and knees, with their elevated hips crossing in the middle in three directions, like the spokes of a wheel, forming a tent-like structure Beneath this protective covering were clustered an heirloom Gila Polychrome basket form, a Chupadero B/w pitcher, and Tonto Polychrome vase, all intact (Figure 35). If these bodies had not already been de-fleshed, they could not have been positioned closely in this manner. A shiny, blackened hairpin, which was lying nearby, is presumed to have fallen from the hair of one of these stacked bodies during the fire.

The floor of Room 101 was evenly covered with fragments of quartz crystal. When heated sufficiently, quartz crystals explode with a loud report. These may have been deliberately placed to dissipate the sacred nature of this important room. Fragments of quartz crystal were also found spread over the roof of an intentionally burned Mimbres great kiva at the Old Town site in New Mexico (Creel and Anyon 2010: 36, Figure 4.7).

Whoever performed these closing activities set fire to the roof supports of the pueblo so that the roofs fell, largely intact. A small polychrome bowl of rabbit and quail stew, and the nests of bowls, came down with the roof without tipping over. A young mother who had been grinding corn on the roof was found still on her knees at her metate, covering the bodies of her toddler and older child with her body. To her right was a jar containing carbonized shelled corn, and at the end of the metate was a bowl containing carbonized finely ground corn meal. To her left was the body of a puppy and brownware miniature dogs with which her children had been playing.

I suspect that the woman and her children in Room 110 were placed as an altar piece, and that the three men who were stacked over important ceramics in Room 102, may have been members of a sodality which made that room its headquarters. These placements may have been intended to restore some sense of order and wholeness to the pueblo. The feasting bowl decorated with the Poorwill mythological motif may have been broken to symbolize the end of the pueblo, like the fall of the southern Big Houses of the past (Rea 2007a: 189).

Where Did The Survivors Go?

Hohmann (personal communication, April 1992) considered lack of wood as more important in the abandonment of the local area than the lack of water. I would add lack of arable land due to canyon ridge erosion, and human infertility caused by eating cottonseed, as contributing factors to Salado disappearance. In the A.D. 1440s, there was still an organized Salado population present at Gila Pueblo. Even after the final attack, there remained a few survivors who knew who the dead had been, and who were able to perform appropriate closing activities and fire the pueblo. Having accomplished this obligation, they had to go somewhere.

If the survivors fled east, they would have moved along a documented historic trail along Gilson Wash to the San Carlos River (Crary, Germick, and Golio 1994: Figure 4). They probably would have found the settlement at Rice deserted. However, they could have continued down the San Carlos River to the Gila, and followed it upstream to a Salado settlement at Thatcher, in the Safford Valley, which persisted into the historic period.

Wallace and Doelle (2001: 263) describe settlements along the lower San Pedro which had compounds and even platform mounds. However, the population dwindled until there were only two villages left in the Dudleyville Sector, perhaps as late as A.D. 1425-1450 (Clark and Lyons 2012: 465). Linguistic connections between the Tepiman and Zuni languages suggest that survivors from these villages may have moved back north (Clark, Hill, Lyons, and Lengyel 2012: 494).

Considering the changes in location of religious artifacts at Gila Pueblo after A.D. 1385, and the kinds of artifacts, it appears that fleeing to what is now Pima territory might have been the preferred choice. These include the large greenstone sphere, the antlered deer cranium, the oval/water drum bowls at Gila Pueblo and Pinal Pueblo, the deer dancer bead made from local argillite, and a Pima-like preference for white-tailed deer over black-tailed deer (Rea 1998: 238- 246). Amadeo Rea's forthcoming publication on Pima migrations may shed light on the matter.

Looking Back on Salado Research

Publications which have become available since the compilation of the site report on Gila Pueblo and the Hagen Site (McKusick and Young 1997) have changed the picture of the late pre-Hispanic period in southeastern Arizona considerably. The facts put forth in *The Gila Pueblo Salado* are still accurate, but their interpretation has matured. The naming of Cliff Polychrome, which was so important in the last days of the Upland Salado pueblos, turns attention toward the south and the east, rather than the north.

Meanwhile, the uplands and the desert continue their cycles from year to year. On Good Friday evening, as I follow the procession of the Stations of the Cross at St John's in Globe, I know that the baptized faithful at Pasqua Village have carried the Three Marys out of the church, and the Deer Dancer has stepped forth once more from the Flower World, to parallel the procession of the Stations of the Cross in Tucson. The earth is renewed again. The more things change, the more things stay the same.

References Cited

Adams, E. Charles
    1991   *The Origin and Development of the Pueblo Katsina Cult.* University of Arizona Press, Tucson.

    2013   Prehispanic Jeddito Yellow Ware: an Overview. *Kiva* 79(2): 105-124.

Adovasio, J. M., Olga Soffer, and Jake Page
    2007   *The Invisible Sex.* Smithsonian Books, New York.

Alvarado, Denise
    2012   *Day of the Dead Handbook.* Creole Moon Publications, Lexington.

Anderson, J. E.
    1969   *The Human Skeleton.* The National Museum of Canada, Ottawa.

Anderson, Keith M., Gloria J. Fenner, Don P. Morris, George A. Teague, and Charmion McKusick
    1986   *The Archeology of Gila Cliff Dwellings.* Western Archeological and Conservation Center Publications in Anthropology 36. National Park Service, U.S. Department of the Interior, Tucson.

Austin, Oliver L. Jr.
    1961   *The Birds of the World.* The Golden Press, Inc., New York

Bernardini, Wesley
    2011   North, South, and Center: An Outline of Hopi Ethnogenesis. In *Religious Transformation in the Late Pre-Hispanic Pueblo World,* edited by Donna M. Glowacki and Scott Van Keuren, pp. 196-220. Amerind Studies in Archaeology, series editor John Ware. University of Arizona Press, Tucson.

Boggess, Doug, Norma Ajeman, Catherine Gilman, and Linda Bozarth
    1992   Incorporating Site Vandalism: An Assessment of Pinal Pueblo. In *Proceedings of the Second Salado Conference, Globe, AZ 1992,* edited by Richard C. Lange and Stephen Germick, pp. 183-190. Occasional Paper of the Arizona Archaeological Society, Phoenix Chapter.

Bohrer, Vorsila L.
    2007   *Preceramic Subsistence in Two Rock Shelters in Fresnal Canyon, South Central New Mexico.* Arizona State Museum Archaeological Series 199. University of Arizona Press, Tucson.

Bolton, Herbert Eugene
    1916   Spanish Exploration in the Southwest. Charles Scribner's Sons, New
             York.

Boone, Elizabeth H., and Michael E. Smith
    2003   Postclassic International Styles and Symbol Sets. In *The Postclassic
             Mesoamerican World,* edited by Michael E. Smith and Frances F. Berdan,
             pp. 186-193. University of Utah Press, Salt Lake City.

Bosveld, Jane
    2009   Brothers in Arms. *Discover,* November 2009, pp. 46-49.

Bradfield, Wesley
    1931   *Cameron Creek Village: A Site in the Mimbres Area in Grant County New
             Mexico.* Monograph of the School of American Research Number 1.

Bradley, Ronna J.
    1999   Shell Exchange within the Southwest. In *The Casas Grandes World,*
             edited by Curtis F. Schaafsma and Carroll L. Riley, pp. 213-228.
             University of Utah Press, Salt Lake City.

Brody, J. J.
    1977   *Mimbres Painted Pottery.* University of New Mexico Press, Albuquerque.

Brody, J. J., Catherine J. Scott, Steven A. LeBlanc, and Tony Berlant
    1983   *Mimbres Pottery: Ancient Art of the American Southwest.* Hudson Hills
             Press, New York.

Brooks, James F.
    2016   *Mesa of Sorrows: A History of the Awat'ovi Massacre.* W. W. Norton &
             Company, New York.

Brown, Cecil H., Eike Luedeling, Søren Wichmann, and Patience Epps
    2013   The Paleobiolinguistics of Domesticated Squash (*Cucurbita* spp.). In
             Explorations in Ethnobiology: The Legacy of Amadeo Rea, edited by
             Marsha Quinlan and Dana Lepofsky, pp. 132-161. Society of
             Ethnobiology, University of Northern Texas, Denton.

Brundage, Burr Catrwright
    1979   *The Fifth Sun, Aztec Gods, Aztec World.* University of Texas Press,
             Austin.

Bullock, Peter Y.
    2007   Ancient DNA and Prehistoric Macaws. *Archaeology Southwest* 21 (1): 6.
             Center for Desert Archaeology, Tucson.

Burland, Cottie, and Werner Forman
    1975   *Feathered Serpent and Smoking Mirror.* Orbis Publishing, London.

Clark, Jeffery J., J. Brett Hill, Patrick D. Lyons, and Stacey N. Lengyel
    2012   Of Migrants and Mounds. In *Migrants and Mounds: Classic Period Archaeology of the Lower San Pedro Valley,* edited by Jeffery J. Clark and Patrick D. Lyons, pp. 345-405. Archaeology Southwest, Anthropological Papers No. 45, Tucson.

Clark, Jeffery J., and Patrick D. Lyons
    2012   Temporal Assignment of Excavated Contexts, San Pedro Preservation Project. In Migrants and Mounds: Classic Period Archaeology of the Lower San Pedro Valley, edited by Jeffery J. Clark and Patrick D. Lyons, pp. 463-467, Archaeology Southwest, Anthropological Papers No. 45, Tucson.

Coe, Michael D.
    1975   Native Astronomy in Mesoamerica. In *Archaeoastronomy in Pre-Columbian America,* edited by Anthony F. Aveni, pp. 3-31. University of Texas Press, Austin.

    2011   *The Maya.* Eighth edition. Thames & Hudson, New York.

Cosgrove, C. B.
    1947   *Caves of the Upper Gila and Hueco Areas in New Mexico and Texas.* Papers of the Peabody Museum of American Archaeology and Ethnology 34(2). Harvard University, Cambridge.

Cosgrove, H. S., and C. B. Cosgrove
    1932   *The Swarts Ruin: A Typical Mimbres Site in Southwestern New Mexico: Report of the Mimbres Valley Expedition Seasons of 1924-1927.* Papers of the Peabody Museum of American Archaeology and Ethnology 15(1). Harvard University, Cambridge.

Crary, Joseph S., Stephen Germick, and Michael Golio
    1994   Late Mogollon Adaptations to the Upper Sonoran Desert: Examples From the Upper Pinal Creek Area, Arizona. In *Mogollon VII: The Collected Papers of the 1992 Mogollon Conference Held in Las Cruces, New Mexico*, pp. 53-65. COAS Publishing & Research, Las Cruces.

Creel, Darrell, and Roger Anyon
    2010   Burning Down the House: Ritual Architecture of the Mimbres Late Pithouse Period. In *Mimbres Lives and Landscape,* edited by Margaret C. Nelson and Michelle Hegmon, pp. 29-37. School for Advanced Research, Santa Fe.

Crosswhite, Frank S.
    1985   *"Xólotl and Quetzalcoatl* in relation to Monstrosities of *Maguey* (Agave)
            and *Teocentli* (Zia), with Notes on the Pre-Columbian Religions of
            Mexico," pp.114-115, and "Agave and Pre-Cortez Religion" pp. 50,
            115,116, *Desert Plants* 7 (2). University of Arizona at the Boyce
            Thompson Southwestern Arboretum, Superior, Arizona.

Crotty, Helen K.
    2001   Shields, Shield Bearers, and Warfare Imagery in Anasazi Art, 1200-1500.
            In *Deadly Landscapes: Case Studies in Prehistoric Warfare.* Edited by
            Glen E. Rice and Steven A. LeBlanc, The University of Utah Press, Salt
            Lake City.

Crown, Patricia L.
    1994   Ceramics and Ideology: Salado Polychrome Pottery. University of New
            Mexico Press, Albuquerque.

Crown, Patricia L., Jiyan Gu, W. Jeffrey Hurst, Timothy J. Ward, Ardith D. Bravenec,
Syed Ali, Laura Kebert, Marlaina Berch, Erin Redman, Patrick D. Lyons, Jamie
Merewether, David A. Phillips, Lori S. Reed, and Kyle Woodson
    2015   Ritual Drinks in the Pre-Hispanic US Southwest and Mexican Northwest.
            *Proceedings of the National Academy of Sciences of the United States of
            America* 112(37):11436-11442. September 15.

Crown, Patricia L., and W. Jeffrey Hurst
    2009   Evidence of Cacao Use in the Prehispanic American Southwest.
            *Proceedings of the National Academy of Sciences of the United States of
            America* 106(7): 2110-2113. February 17.

Cummings, Byron
    1940   *Kinishba: A Prehistoric Pueblo of the Great Pueblo Period.* Hohokam
            Museums Association and the University of Arizona, Tucson.

Curry, Andres
    2007   The Dawn of Art. *Archaeology,* September/October 2007, pp. 28-33.

Davis, Carolyn O'Bagy
    1995   *Treasured Earth: Hattie Cosgrove's Mimbres Archaeology in the
            American Southwest.* Sanpete Publications, and Old Pueblo Archaeology
            Center, Tucson.

Day, Jane S.
    1992   *Aztec.* Denver Museum of Natural History, Denver.

de la Habra, Louis
   1976   Clues to America's Past. The National Geographic Society, Washington, D.C.

Di Peso, Charles C.
   1974   *Casas Grandes: A Fallen Trading Center of the Gran Chichimeca, Vol. 2, Medio Period.* The Amerind Foundation 9. Dragoon, Arizona.

Ellison, Peter T.
   2001   *On Fertile Ground: A Natural History of Human Reproduction.* Harvard University Press, Cambridge.

Evers, Larry, and Felipe S. Molina
   1987   *Yaqui Deer Songs: Maso Bwikam.* Sun Tracks, Volume 14. University of Arizona Press, Tucson.

Feher-Elston, Catherine.
   1991 Ravensong. Northland Publishing, Flagstaff.

Fenner, Gloria J.
   1974a   Carretas Polychrome Decoration. In *Casas Grandes: A Fallen Trading Center of the Gran Chichimecs, Vol. 6, Ceramics and Shell,* by Charles C. Di Peso, John B. Rinaldo, and Gloria J. Fenner, pp. 200-206. The Amerind Foundation 9. Dragoon, Arizona.

   1974b   Huerigos Polychrome Decoration. In *Casas Grandes: A Fallen Trading Center of the Gran Chichimecs, Vol. 6, Ceramics and Shell,* by Charles C. Di Peso, John B. Rinaldo, and Gloria J. Fenner, pp. 245-250. The Amerind Foundation 9. Dragoon, Arizona.

Ferg, Alan
   1982   14th Century Kachina Depictions on Ceramics. In *Collected Papers in Honor of John W. Runyan,* edited by Gerald X. Fitzgerald, pp. 13-29. *Papers of the Archaeological Society of New Mexico 7.* Albuquerque Archaeological Society Press.

   1988   Appendix E: Exotic Artifacts and Shrines. In *Erich F. Schmidt's Investigations of Salado Sites in Central Arizona,* edited by John W. Hohmann and Linda B. Kelly, pp. 205-218. Museum of Northern Arizona Bulletin 56. Flagstaff.

Fisher, Richard D.
   2003   *Copper Canyon.* Sunracer Publications, Tucson.

Fulton, William Shirley, and Carr Tuthill
1945   *An Archaeological Site Near Gleeson, Arizona.* The Amerind Foundation 1. Dragoon, Arizona.

Furst, Peter T.
1972   To Find Our Life: Peyote Among the Huichol Indians of Mexico. In *Flesh of the Gods: the Ritual Use of Hallucinogens,* edited by Peter T. Furst, pp.136-184. Praeger Publishers, New York.

Gavan, James A.
1940   Physical Anthropology of Besh-ba-gowah. *The Kiva* 6(3): 9-12.

Gifford, Edward W.
1940   Culture Element Distributions XII: Apache-Pueblo. *University of California, Anthropological Record,* Volume 4, Number 1.

Gonzales, Patrisia
2012   *Red Medicine: Traditional Indigenous Rites of Birthing and Healing.* University of Arizona Press, Tucson.

Gregory, David A., and Wilcox, David R.
2008   "Zuni Language Distribution." *Archaeology Southwest,* Volume 22, Number 2, Tucson.

Griffen, P. Bion
1967   "A High Status Burial from Grasshopper Ruin, Arizona." The Kiva 33(2): 37-53.

Hammond, George P., and Agapito Rey
1940   Narratives of the Coronado Expedition, 1540-1542. Coronado Cuarto-Centennial Publication, Vol. 2. University of New Mexico Press, Albuquerque.

Haury, Emil W.
1934   *The Canyon Creek Ruin and the Cliff Dwellings of the Sierra Ancha.* Medallion Papers 14. Gila Pueblo Foundation, Globe, Arizona.

1937   Stone: Palettes and Ornaments. In *Excavations at Snaketown: Material Culture,* by Harold S. Gladwin, Emil W. Haury, E. B. Sayles, and Nora Gladwin, pp. 121-134. Medallion Papers 25. Gila Pueblo Foundation, Globe, Arizona.

1958   Evidence at Point of Pines for a Prehistoric Migration from Northern Arizona. In *Migrations in New World Cultural History,* edited by Raymond H. Thompson, pp. 1-6. University of Arizona Bulletin 29(2), Social Science Bulletin 27. Tucson.

1975   *The Stratigraphy and Archaeology of Ventana Cave.* New edition. University of Arizona Press, Tucson.

1976   *The Hohokam: Desert Farmers & Craftsmen. Excavations at Snaketown, 1964-1965.* University of Arizona Press, Tucson.

Hayden, Brian
    1990   Nimrods, Piscators, Pluckers, and Planters: The Emergence of Food Production. *Journal of Anthropological Archaeology* 9: 31-69.

Hayes, Alden C., Jon Nathan Young, and A. H. Warren
    1981   *Excavation of Mound 7.* Archaeological Research Series No. 16. National Park Service, Washington, D.C.

Hays-Gilpin, Kelley
    2006   Icons and Ethnicity: Hopi Painted Pottery and Murals. In *Religion in the Prehispanic Southwest,* edited by Christine S. VanPool, Todd L. VanPool, and David A. Phillips, Jr., pp. 67-80. AltaMira Press, Lanham, Maryland.

Hays-Gilpin, Kelley, Emory Sekaquaptewa, and Elizabeth A. Newsome
    2010   "Siitalpuva, 'Through the Land Brightened with Flowers': Ecology and Cosmology in Mural and Pottery Painting, Hopi and Beyond". In *Painting the Cosmos: Metaphor and Worldview in Images from the Southwest Pueblo and Mexico,* edited by Kelly Hays-Gilpin and Polly Schaafsma. Museum of Northern Arizona Bulletin 67, Flagstaff.

Herr, Sarah H.
    2009   The Latest Research on the Earliest Farmers. *Archaeology Southwest* 23(1): 1-3. Center for Desert Archaeology, Tucson.

Hinkes, Madeliene J. M.
    1996   Wind Mountain Osteological Analysis. In *Mimbres Mogollon Archaeology,* edited by Anne I. Woosley and Allan J. McIntyre, pp. 373-388. The Amerind Foundation 10. University of New Mexico Press, Albuquerque.

Hohmann, John W.
    1990   *Ruin Stabilization and Park Development for Besh-Ba-Gowah Pueblo.* Studies in Western Archaeology Number 1, Cultural Resource Group, Louis Berger & Associates, Inc., Phoenix.

    1992a *Through the Mirror of Death: A View of Prehistoric Social Complexity in Central Arizona.* Doctoral dissertation, Department of Anthropology, Arizona State University, Tempe.

1992b   An Overview of Salado Heartland Archaeology. In *Proceedings of the Second Salado Conference,* edited by Richard C. Lange and Stephen Germick., pp.1-16. Arizona Archaeological Society Occasional Paper, Phoenix.

Hohmann, John W., and Christopher D. Adams
1992   Salado Site Configuration and Growth: The Besh-Ba-Gowah Example. In Proceedings *of the Second Salado Conference, Globe, AZ 1992,* edited by Richard C. Lange and Stephen Germick, pp. 109-124. Occasional Paper of the Arizona Archaeological Society, Phoenix Chapter.

Hohmann, John W., Paul Fortin, Jerry Howard, and Helen O'Brien
1985   Site AZ U:3:49 (ASU). In *Hohokam and Salado Hamlets in the Tonto Basin: Site Descriptions,* by John W. Hohmann, pp. 216-290. OCRM Report Number 64. Office of Cultural Resource Management, Arizona State University, Tempe.

Hohmann, John W., Stephen Germick, and Christopher D. Adams
1992   Discovery of a Salado Ceremonial Room. In *Proceedings of the Second Salado Conference, Globe, AZ 1992,* edited by Richard C. Lange and Stephen Germick, pp. 92-102. Occasional Paper of the Arizona Archaeological Society, Phoenix Chapter.

Holliday, Vance T., Michael Bever, and David J. Meltzer
2009   Paleoindians in the American Southwest and Northern Mexico. Archaeology Southwest 23(3): 1-3.

Huckell, Lisa W., and Christine S. VanPool
2006   *Toloatzin* and Shamanic Journeys: Exploring the Ritual Role of Sacred Datura in the Prehistoric Southwest. In *Religion in the Prehispanic Southwest,* edited by Christine S. VanPool, Todd L. VanPool, and David A. Phillips, Jr., pp. 147-163. AltaMira Press, Lanham, Maryland.

Koerper, Henry C., Galen Hunter, Ivan Snyder, and Joe Cramer
2014   "Marine Mammal Ear Bones as Charms/Curiosities," *Pacific Coast Archaeological Society Quarterly,* Volume 49, Numbers 1 and 2.

Koerper, Henry C. and Jere H. Kipps
2015   "Additional Evidence of Marine Mammal Middle Ear Bones as Special Objects". *Pacific Coast Archaeological Society Quarterly,* Volume 51, Number 2.

Le Blanc, Steven A.
1999   *Prehistoric Warfare in the American Southwest.* The University of Utah Press,   Salt Lake City.

Le Blanc, Steven A., Lori S. Cobb Kreisman, Brian M. Kemp, et al.
2007   Quids and Aprons: Ancient DNA from the American Southwest. *Journal of Field Archaeology* 32 (2):161-75).

Lekson, Stephen H., Curtis P. Nepstad-Thornberry, Brian E. Yunker, Toni S. Laumbach, David P. Cain, and Karl W. Laumbach
2002   Migrations in the Southwest: Pinnacle Ruin, Southwestern New Mexico. *Kiva* 68(2): 73-101.

Lindauer, Owen
1996   "Understanding the Salado Through Work at Schoolhouse Point Platform Mound," UL:8:24/13A, pp. 841-858. In Owen Lindauer et al, *The Place of the Storehouses: Roosevelt Platform Mound Study.* Roosevelt Monograph Series 6, Anthropological Field Studies 35, Arizona State University, Tempe.

Lobell, Jarrett A., and Eric A. Powell
2010   More than Man's Best Friend. Archaeology, September/October 2010, pp. 26-35.

Luckert, Karl W.
1975   *The Navajo Hunter Tradition.* University of Arizona Press, Tucson.

Lyons, Patrick D.
2004   José Solas Ruin. *Kiva* 70(2): 143-181.

Lyons, Patrick D., and Alexander J. Lindsay, Jr.
2006   Perforated Plates and the Salado Phenomenon. *Kiva* 72(1): 5-54.

Malakoff, David
2008   Rethinking the Clovis. *American Archaeology 12*(4): 26-31. Winter 2008-09.

Marshack, Alexander
n.d.   *Ice Age Art.* The Academy of Natural Sciences of Philadelphia in Cooperation with the Smith Kline Foundation.

1988   An Ice Age Ancestor? *National Geographic* 174(4): 478-481. October.

Martin, Debra L.
2000   Bodies and Lives. In *Women & Men in the Prehispanic Southwest: Labor, Power & Prestige,* edited by Patricia L. Crown, pp. 267-300. School of American Research Advanced Seminar Series, Santa Fe.

McGregor, John C.
　　1965　*Southwestern Archaeology.* Second edition. Southern Illinois University Press, Urbana.

McGuire, Randall H.
　　2011　Pueblo Religion and the Mesoamerican Connection. In *Religious Transformation in the Late Pre-Hispanic World,* edited by Donna M. Glowacki and Scott Van Keuren, pp. 23-49. University of Arizona Press, Tucson.

McKusick, Charmion R.
　　1974　The Casas Grandes Avian Report. In *Casas Grandes, A Fallen Trading Center of the Gran Chichimeca,* Volume 8, By Charles C. DiPeso, John B. Rinaldo, and Gloria J. Fenner, pp. 373-284. Amerind Foundation, Dragoon.

　　1976.　Avifauna. In *The Hohokam: Desert Farmers and Craftsmen. Excavations at Snaketown,* 1964-1965, by Emil W. Haury, pp 374-377. University of Arizona Press, Tucson.

　　1982　Avifauna from Grasshopper Pueblo. In *Multidisciplinary Research at Grasshopper Pueblo, Arizona,* edited by William A. Longacre, Sally J. Holbrook, and Michael W. Graves, pp. 87-96. Anthropological Papers of the University of Arizona 40. University of Arizona Press, Tucson.

　　1986　*Southwest Indian Turkeys: Prehistory and Comparative Osteology.* Southwest Bird Laboratory, Globe, Arizona.

　　1992　Evidences of Hereditary High Status at Gila Pueblo. In *Proceedings of the Second Salado Conference, Globe, AZ 1992,* edited by Richard C. Lange and Stephen Germick, pp. 86-91. Occasional Paper of the Arizona Archaeological Society, Phoenix Chapter.

　　2001　*Southwest Birds of Sacrifice.* The Arizona Archaeologist 31. Arizona Archaeological Society, Phoenix.

　　2013　Upland Salado Resource Use. In *Explorations in Ethnobiology: The Legacy of Amadeo Rea,* edited by Marsha Quinlan and Dana Lepofsky, pp. 272-296. Society of Ethnobiology, University of North Texas, Denton.

McKusick, Charmion R., and Jon Nathan Young
　　1997　*The Gila Pueblo Salado.* Salado Chapter, Arizona Archaeological Society, Globe, Arizona.

Miller, Mary, and Karl Taube
    1993   *The Gods and Symbols of Ancient Mexico and the Maya.* Thames & Hudson, London.

Moulard, Barbara L.
    1981   *Within the Underworld Sky: Mimbres Ceramic Art in Context.* Twelvetrees Press, Pasadena, California.

Mone, Gregory
    2012   Things You Didn't Know about Sex. *Discover,* June 2012, p. 72.

Müller-Ebeling, Claudia, Christian Rätsch, Surendra Bahadur Shahi
    2000   *Shamanism and Tantra in the Himalayas.* Translated by Anabel Lee. Inner Traditions, Rochester, Vermont.

Nabhan, Gary Paul
    2004   *Cross-pollinations: The Marriage of Science and Poetry.* Milkweed Editions, Minneapolis.

Neimark, Jill
    2011   Meet the New Human Family. *Discover,* May 2010, pp. 48-55.

Neithammer, Carolyn
    1974   *American Indian Cooking.* University of Nebraska Press, Lincoln.

Oates, Shani
    2011   *Tubelo's Green Fire.* Mandrake of Oxford.

Oroc, James
    2009   *Tryptamine Palace.* Park Street Press, Rochester, Vermont.

Papagianni, Dimitra, and Michael A. Morse
    2013   *The Neanderthals Rediscovered.* Thames & Hudson, London.

Parsons, Elsie Clews
    1939   *Pueblo Indian Religion.* University of Chicago Press, Chicago.

Patel, Samir S.
    2011   World Roundup: Spain. *Archaeology,* March/April 2011, pp.14-15.

Peigler, Richard S.
    1994   Non-Sericultural Uses of Moth Cocoons in Diverse Cultures. Proceedings of the Denver Museum of Natural History 3(5): 1-20. July 1.

Pendell, Dale
    2009   Pharmako Gnosis: Plant Teachers and the Poison Path. North American
            Books, Berkeley, California.

Phillips, David A., Jr., Christine S. VanPool, and Todd L. VanPool
    2006   The Horned Serpent Tradition in the North American Southwest. In
            Religion in the Prehispanic Southwest, edited by Christine S. VanPool,
            Todd L. VanPool, and David A. Phillips, Jr., pp. 17-29. AltaMira Press,
            Lanham, Maryland.

Pilles, Peter J., and Edward B. Danson
    1974   The Prehistoric Pottery of Arizona. *Arizona Highways* 50(2): 2-5, 10-32.
            February.

Prideaux, Tom
    1973   *Cro-Magnon Man.* Time-Life Books, New York.

Pringle, Heather
    2010   Battle for the Xinjiang Mummies. *Archaeology* 63(4): 170-180.
            July/August.

Rätsch, Christian
    1998   *The Encyclopedia of Psychoactive Plants.* Translated by John R. Baker.
            Park Street Press, Rochester, Vermont.

Rea, Amadeo M.
    1997   *At the Desert's Green Edge: An Ethnobotany of the Gila River Pima.*
            University of Arizona Press, Tucson.

    1998   *Folk Mammalogy of the Northern Pimans.* University of Arizona Press,
            Tucson.

    2007a *Wings in the Desert: A Folk Ornithology of the Northern Pimans.*
            University of Arizona Press, Tucson.

    2007b The Poorwill in Pima Oral Traditions. *Archaeology Southwest* 21(1): 7.
            Center for Desert Archaeology, Tucson.

Reid, Jefferson, and Stephanie Whittlesey
    1999   *Grasshopper Pueblo: A Story of* Archaeology *and Ancient Life.* University
            of Arizona Press, Tucson.

Rice, Glen E., and Charles L. Redman
    1992   Power in the Past. *Native Peoples Magazine* 5(4): 18-25. Summer.

Roney, John, and Robert Hard
      2009   The Beginnings of Maize Agriculture. *Archaeology Southwest* 23(1): 4-5.

Schaafsma, Polly (editor)
      1994   *Kachinas in the Pueblo World.* University of New Mexico Press,
                   Albuquerque.

      2000   *Kachinas in the Pueblo World.* University of Utah Press, Salt Lake City.

Schultes, Richard Evans
      1972   An Overview of Hallucinogens in the Western Hemisphere. In *Flesh of the
                   Gods,* edited by Peter T. Furst, 3-54. Praeger Publishers, New York.

Schultes, Richard Evans, Albert Hofmann, and Christian Rätsch
      2001   *Plants of the Gods: Their Sacred, Healing, and Hallucinogenic Powers.*
                   Healing Arts Press, Rochester, Vermont.

Schuster, Carl, and Edmund Carpenter
      1996   *Patterns that Connect.* Harry N. Abrams, Inc., Publishers, New York.

Scott, G. Richard
      1981   A Stature Reconstruction of Skeletal Population. In *Contributions to Gran
                   Quivira Archeology, Gran Quivira National Monument, New Mexico,*
                   edited by Alden C. Hayes, pp. 129-137. Publications in Archeology 17.
                   National Park Service, U.S. Department of the Interior, Washington, D.C.

Shafer, Harry J.
      2003   *Archaeology at the NAN Ranch Ruin.* University of New Mexico Press,
                   Albuquerque.

Sheridan, Thomas E., and Nancy J. Parezo (editors)
      1996   *Paths of Life: American Indians of the Southwest and Northern Mexico.*
                   University of Arizona Press, Tucson.

Shiner, Joel L.
      1961   A Room at Gila Pueblo. *The Kiva* 27(2): 3-11.

Smith, Philip G.
      1979   Salado Sites in the Dripping Springs Valley, Central Arizona. *The Artifact*
                   17(2): 37-69.

Smith, Watson
      1952   *Kiva Mural Decorations at Awatovi and Kawaika-a, With a Survey of
                   Other Wall Paintings in the Pueblo Southwest.* Papers of the Peabody
                   Museum of American Archaeology and Ethnology 37. Harvard
                   University, Cambridge.

Smith, Watson, Richard B. Woodbury, and Nathalie F. S. Woodbury
    1966   *The Excavation of Hawikuh by Frederick Webb Hodge; Report of the Hendricks-Hodge Expedition, 1917-1923*. Contributions From the Museum of the American Indian, Heye Foundation 20. Museum of the American Indian, Heye Foundation, New York.

Stephen, Alexander M.
    1936   Hopi Journal of Alexander M. Stephen. Edited by Elsie Clews Parsons. Columbia University Contributions to Anthropology 23. Columbia University Press, New York.

Stevenson, Matilda Coxe
    1904   The Zuni Indians: Their Mythology, Esoteric Fraternities, and Ceremonies. Twenty-Third Annual Report of the Bureau of American Ethnology to the Secretary of the Smithsonian, 1901-1902, pp. 1-634. Washington, D.C.: Smithsonian Institution.

Stone, Andrea, and Marc Zender
    2011   *Reading Maya Art: A Hieroglyphic Guide to Ancient Maya Painting and Sculpture*. Thames & Hudson, New York.

Stone, Richard
    2001   *Mammoth*. Perseus Publishing, Cambridge, Massachusetts.

Storer, Tracy I.
    1943   *General Zoology*. McGraw-Hill Book Company, Inc., New York.

Taube, Karl
    2010   Gateways to Another World: The Symbolism of Supernatural Passageways in the Art and Ritual of Mesoamerica and the American Southwest. In Painting the Cosmos: Metaphor and Worldview in Images from the Southwest Pueblos and Mexico. Edited by Kelley Hayes-Gilpin and Polly Schaafsma, Museum of Northern Arizona Bulletin 67.

Thompson, Marc
    2006   Pre-Columbian Venus: Celestial Twin and Icon of Duality. In *Religion in the Prehispanic Southwest,* edited by Christine S. VanPool, Todd L. VanPool, and David A. Phillips, Jr., pp. 165-183. AltaMira Press, Lanham, Maryland.

Time-Life Books
    1995   *Early Europe: Mysteries in Stone*. Richmond, Virginia.

Underhill, Ruth M.
  1965   *Red Man's Religion; Beliefs and Practices of the Indians North of Mexico.*
         University of Chicago Press, Chicago.

Vaillant, George C.
  1950   *Aztecs of Mexico.* Doubleday and Company, Garden City.

VanPool, Christine S. and Todd L. VanPool
  2007   *Signs of the Casas Grandes Shamans.* University of Utah Press, Salt Lake
         City.

van Renterghem, Tony
  1995   *When Santa was a Shaman.* Llewellyn Publications, St. Paul.

Vickrey, Irene S.
  1939   Besh-ba-gowah. *The Kiva* 4(5): 19-22.

  1945   Inspiration I. *The Kiva 10*(3): 22-28.

Vitebsky, Piers
  2005   *The Reindeer People.* Houghton Mifflin Company, New York.

Vivian, R. Gwinn, Dulce N. Dodgen, and Gayle H. Hartmann
  1978   *Wooden Ritual Artifacts from Chaco Canyon, New Mexico. The Chetro Ketl
         Collection.* Anthropological Papers of the University of Arizona 32.
         University of Arizona Press, Tucson.

Vokes, Arthur W., and David A. Gregory
  2007   Exchange Networks for Exotic Goods in the Southwest and Zuni's Place
         in Them. In *Zuni Origins: Toward a New Synthesis of Southwestern
         Archaeology,* edited by David A. Gregory and David R. Wilcox, pp. 318-
         357. University of Arizona Press, Tucson.

Wallace, Henry D., and William H. Doelle
  2001   Classic Period. In *Deadly Landscapes: Case Studies in Prehistoric
         Southwestern Warfare,* edited by Glen E. Rice and Steven A. LeBlanc, pp.
         239-287. University of Utah Press, Salt Lake City.

Warren, Bruce W., and Thomas Stuart Ferguson
  1987   *The Messiah in Ancient America.* Book of Mormon Research Foundation,
         Provo.

Weil, Andrew
  1980   *The Marriage of the Sun and the Moon.* Houghton Mifflin, Boston.

Wheat, Joe Ben
    1967   A Paleo-Indian Bison Kill. *Scientific American* 216(1): 44-52.

White, Leslie A.
    1962   *The Pueblo of Sia, New Mexico.* Bureau of American Ethnology Bulletin 184.

Whittaker, John C., Alan Ferg, and John Speth
    1988   Arizona Bifaces of Wyoming Chert. *The Kiva* 53(4): 321-334.

Wilcox, David R., Gerald Robertson, Jr., and J. Scott Wood
    2001   Organized for War: The Perry Mesa Settlement System and Its Central Arizona Neighbors. In *Deadly Landscapes: Case Studies in Prehistoric Southwestern Warfare,* edited by Glen E. Rice and Steven A. LeBlanc, pp. 41-194. University of Utah Press, Salt Lake City.

Wilcox, David R., David A. Gregory, and J. Brett Hill
    2009   "Zuni in the Pueblo and Southwestern World," in *Zuni Origins: Toward a New Synthesis in Southwestern Archaeology,* edited by David A. Gregory and David R. Wilcox, pp. 165-209. The University of Arizona Press, Tucson

Williams, J. S., T. J. Blackhorse, J. R. Stein, and R. Friedman
    2006   *Iikááh:* Chaco Sacred Schematics. In *Religion in the Prehispanic Southwest,* edited by Christine S. VanPool, Todd L. VanPool, and David A. Phillips, Jr., pp.103-113. Altimira Press, Lanham, Maryland.

Wood, J. Scott
    1986   Vale of Tiers: Tonto Basin in the 14th Century. Paper presented at the 59th Pecos Conference, Payson, Arizona.

    1987   *Checklist of Pottery Types for the Tonto National Forest.* The Arizona Archaeologist 21. Arizona Archaeological Society, Phoenix.

Wood, J. Scott, Martin E. McAllister, and Michael A. Sullivan
    1989   *11,000 Years on the Tonto National Forest.* Southwest Natural and Cultural Heritage Association, Albuquerque, New Mexico, and Tonto National Forest.

Young, Jon Nathan
    1967   *The Salado Culture in Southwestern Prehistory.* Doctoral dissertation, University of Arizona, Tucson. University Microfilms, Ann Arbor.

Young, M. Jane

    1994   The Interconnection between Western Puebloan and Mesoamerican Ideology/Cosmology. In *Kachinas in the Pueblo World,* edited by Polly Schaafsma, pp. 107-120. University of New Mexico Press, Albuquerque.

    2000   The Interconnection between Western Puebloan and Mesoamerican Ideology/Cosmology. In *Kachinas in the Pueblo World,* edited by Polly Schaafsma, pp. 107-120. University of Utah Press, Salt Lake City.

Zimmerman, Nancy

    2013   Puebloan Polychrome. *American Archaeology* 17(1): 20-25. The Archaeological Conservancy, Albuquerque.

68020853R00095

Made in the USA
San Bernardino, CA
30 January 2018